Almost Perfect

Advance Praise

'Erika is passion, grit and determination incarnate. Those who think these qualities are innate will be surprised when they read this inspiring book'.

—**Guy Laliberté**, Founder of Cirque du Soleil and Groupe Lune Rouge, recognized by *Time Magazine* as one of the 100 most influential people in the world

'*Almost Perfect* is a unique story that we can all learn from. It is a collection of advice applicable to your professional and personal life'.

—**Daniel Lamarre**, CEO and President Cirque Du Soleil

'*Almost Perfect* brings us behind the scenes, where everyone falls and gets back on their feet. Erika Lemay is such an ethereal creature and strong personality. She made her dream come true with passion, talent, and determination. A great lesson for all of us in these hard times'.

—**Cristina Lucchini**, Co-Editor *Vanity Fair Italia*

'Erika Lemay is the poster child for extreme discipline and dedication to her craft. Her constant quest for perfection makes her admirable and endearing. Now with her new book *Almost Perfect* she inspires us to reach for the highest goals and dreams'.

—**Douglas and Francoise Kirkland**, Photographer

'Erika Lemay shares the secrets of excellence and success in her inspiring story. While this path is a very personal and solitary one, any person striving to make a difference in the world has confronted the very same questions, doubts, mistakes, and feelings of self-overestimation and underestimation. *Almost Perfect* portrays the very essence of the artist and, in general, of the overachiever who discovers the inevitable truth: perfecting oneself is not a "coveted destination, but an eternal direction"'.

—**Maestro Alvise Casellati**, Conductor

Almost Perfect

THE LIFE GUIDE TO
*Creating Your Success Story Through
Passion and Fearlessness*

Erika Lemay

NEW YORK

LONDON • NASHVILLE • MELBOURNE • VANCOUVER

Almost Perfect

The Life Guide to Creating Your Success Story Through Passion and Fearlessness

© 2022 Erika Lemay

Published in New York, New York, by Morgan James Publishing. Morgan James is a trademark of Morgan James, LLC. www.MorganJamesPublishing.com

A **FREE** ebook edition is available for you or a friend with the purchase of this print book.

CLEARLY SIGN YOUR NAME ABOVE

Instructions to claim your free ebook edition:
1. Visit MorganJamesBOGO.com
2. Sign your name CLEARLY in the space above
3. Complete the form and submit a photo of this entire page
4. You or your friend can download the ebook to your preferred device

ISBN 9781631954252 paperback
ISBN 9781631954269 ebook
Library of Congress Control Number: 2020950483

Cover and Interior Design by:
Chris Treccani
www.3dogcreative.net

Cover and Photography by:
Douglas Kirkland all rights reserved

Morgan James is a proud partner of Habitat for Humanity Peninsula and Greater Williamsburg. Partners in building since 2006.

Get involved today! Visit
MorganJamesPublishing.com/giving-back

To those who told me to give up.

Table of Contents

Introduction

Catalyst

PHOTOGRAPHY: JAN DE KONING

Midway through my eight-minute routine, I can feel the audience on the edge of their seat.

I'm half of a second early on the music, so I'll be able to enjoy the next moment, slow down, and show off my skills.

The stage is huge, with enormous video background screens behind me. My live image is projected on the side screens, so even those seated in the back of the auditorium can witness the details of my performance. Everything is exposed: my facial expressions, my contracting muscles, my sweating hands.

Up on my apparatus—three thin, long sticks—I look at the audience. I gather as much air as possible into my lungs for the next contortion that barely allows me to breathe. One of the extreme signature acrobatic movements I'm famous for.

Perfectly coordinated with the piano note, my feet take off. I'm still fully in control and move with ease, balancing above the ground on thin metal canes. My hands poised on small circles of plexiglass built to fit the exact width of my palms. I slowly bring my feet completely to the other side of my body, floating. No gravity. This contortion requires extreme shoulder strength as they support all of my weight whilst in full overextension.

My weight oscillates a little bit towards the left hand. To keep my balance, I constantly lose and regain it ever so slightly. It's the equilibrium concept.

All of a sudden, my left shoulder articulation cedes under me, no longer belonging to the movement. Breaking the line; breaking the rules. The crack resonates in my guts, outplays the music. My elbow is mechanically forced to bend without me having ordered so. It's the first time in my career that my body does what it wants without my command. I am propelled like a rag doll; other limbs, usually graceful, follow the core of my body down to the floor.

On my back, facing the background screens, I don't feel my left upper body the way I usually do. I gaze at my left shoulder and don't like what I see.

Three thoughts pass through my head, in chronological order, in a matter of seconds:

The audience must have noticed.

I've had an incredible stage career.

I am deformed. Will I now be handicapped?

The music keeps playing as I lay on the floor; seconds seem like an eternity. The blue and amber projectors are still hitting my acrobatic props, though my body now lays in the dark. My right hand holds my left shoulder as if it wanted to protect it from something that has already happened. I'm conscious; too conscious. My usual prompt reactiveness has no purpose in this situation. Only a feeling of shame for not having been up to expectations, for not having been perfect, for my deformed body, for the mistake I may have made, for being breakable. A concept I did not know could apply to me.

I stand up, grab my numb left arm with my right hand like a disposable good, and walk gracefully offstage, left exit, making my right side face the audience to spare them the horrible spectacle.

The next six weeks would be intense. Five countries, several surgeons, orthopaedic doctors, therapists, scars, fear, pain—especially psychological. Six incredibly long weeks as, for the first time in my life, I wouldn't rehearse every day, prepare for the next show, focus on perfecting one piece or another or simply my appearance. No one was waiting for me onstage. No one was waiting for me offstage.

I had never felt as lost and lonely as I did then. Through all my difficulties, my Art had always been a loyal companion. I had given my life and soul to it since the age of four. It was not a job or something I did to earn money or fame. It was part of me; it had become my identity.

Had this part of my being been destroyed simultaneously with the tendons, cartilage, and ligaments?

That night, after my shoulder was put back in its socket, I began addressing the next steps of this life episode. I did not know at the time the damage revealed by the MRI would be so important, but I was aware it was not an ordinary injury. My chauffeur drove me back to the apartment I was staying in. During the four-hour ride, with ice on my shoulder, I had time to reflect, to go through all the 'what-ifs'.

I am calm, surprisingly serene, and in solution-mode thinking.

I start writing. Not about the present feelings, not about the past, but about my future.

I don't yet have a precise diagnosis, but I know something has changed, and I'll never physically and psychologically be the same. The glue I have applied to my body for years to keep the pieces together had suddenly let go, and some pieces were lost forever.

I write down my new priorities, new goals, new structure of my days. All the positive outcomes I can come up with. The silver lining in time of chaos and shock.

I have given my whole life to one passion, made it my priority, my reason why, my first love, the influencer of my daily choices. I have been touring the world for 24 years, I'm recognised worldwide, and have a strong business, based only on my being onstage, showing what's possible. I express myself through this very vocation. I've learned most of my emotional and practical patterns through it. This Art, my *Physical Poetry*, is my language; it's my everyday teacher.

I've never stopped training for more than 11 days in a row in my entire life. This accident is, to everyone who knows me, a disaster.

PART 1

Foundation

Chapter 1

Hungry

———————————

Only those with a real thirst
for success will stand out.

Take two perfectly healthy and physically identical young girls, with the same chances—equal body capacities to start with, competent teachers, the same number of hours of training, and loving families. Why will one become a champion, the one-in-a-million, whilst the other one will remain in the mass and only become good? Why does one migrate from good-to great-land? The real question is: how does one go from great to outstanding? The answer might reside in several different factors, but one of them is decisive.

I wasn't particularly talented, and I was neither strong nor powerful. I was skinny with an ineffective physique. My legs being disproportionally long for my trunk; there were basic movements I could simply not achieve for this reason. But I had a secret weapon. Something I used as a tool from a very young age to become the best at whatever I put my head into. *I wanted more than anyone else.*

At four years old, I had my first classical dance class in the small town I come from in Canada, Saint-Étienne-de-Lauzon, with many other clumsy little girls. It wasn't particularly challenging, so I quickly rose in the hierarchy of the tiny ballerinas, landing in a class of 12-year-olds when I was seven.

The end of season recitals was a treat. I loved the stage as soon as I put my feet on it. The blinding projectors were never intimidating. If I could have changed the choreography, making me the only lead dancer in the centre and the other children behind, or even backstage, I would have.

With the focus I applied to it, I learned faster than the others. As I progressed, ballet soon became unchallenging, lacking adrenaline. My goal of becoming a prima ballerina was losing its once appealing character.

At eight years old with a failed attempt at swimming lessons— my lips turned blue in a matter of minutes—I met artistic gymnastics. I soon decided I would go to the Olympics. I wasn't a good gymnast; my proportions were wrong for the sport. I was too tall, too flimsy, and too old. Some five-year-olds were already doing what I was desperately attempting to learn, but I spent every second of my waking hours trying to improve.

With my will and work, I made it to an acceptable level—to say it politely—convinced coaches that I deserved to be put in a better class so I could train four days a week instead of three. I doubt there was a girl in that gymnasium who wanted more than me. My commitment to improving had no boundaries.

Even as an eight-year-old, I'd sermonise my parents for not putting me to bed by 8 p.m. *I had school and gymnastics the next day. How would I perform without sleeping properly?* I was not 100% aware of my flaws; otherwise, I doubt I'd have pushed so much. Sometimes, naivety and ignorance are a good thing. I was placed in an advanced group. Almost every day after school, my parents would drive me to my three-hour training. I'd come back covered in white powder from the magnesium 'chalk' used to absorb sweat and increase my grip. I was hoping for blisters because of the uneven bars; in my mind, that would have been a sign of real commitment and made me a legitimate gymnast. I craved hard work, and I wanted more. My trainer was not as motivated as I was, and that became the norm for me throughout all my learning experiences. I took charge as much as possible even though I was a beginner.

In my new, levelled-up group, where I was undoubtedly the least talented—read between the lines: experienced—I met Karine. Three years my senior but exactly my height and a better-built body, Karine looked like a gymnast and not a weak stick. We became training buddies and later, also phone pals during the nights without gymnastics. Even as a child, I was always more attracted to older, wiser human beings. I loved to learn, and I quickly felt unchallenged and bored with everything I did. Karine was 'cool', and for some reason, she liked to spend time with me in the locker rooms after training and talk to me in between the series when the coach wasn't watching. Typically, no one likes to hang out with the gymnast who can't even nail the basics. It's shameful.

During the fall of 1994, at a Saturday morning gymnastics session, Karine mentioned a circus troupe she was training with on weekends, led by Michel Rousseau, aka clown Popof. A few acrobats from Quebec City would teach kids in Karine's home town, a few kilometres from mine, even deeper into the countryside.

Acrobats? I had to go!

The following Saturday, I had my circus initiation in a town called Saint-Lambert-de-Lauzon in an under-equipped school gymnasium. The director invited the two of us to practice with the circus artists the next day. Their training venue was in Quebec City, and they were the best in the region, he said.

I had no hesitation, only to convince my parents.

SUNDAY AT THE CIRCUS

Karine and I arrived early for our day of discovery, dressed as gymnasts, completely mismatched with the mood of the place. I kept a baggy T-shirt and my socks on the entire day, ashamed of revealing I only wore a mini-leotard. I had a contortion class, acrobatics class, trapeze, monocycle. I was terrible at everything but in awe of what was happening around me. These circus acrobats not only were out-of-this-world amazing, but they were all so different from one another. As if the highest special skills of the world were united in the same room. They were all physically different as well, which is abnormal for any sport, where athletes usually have similar physical attributes. But that's precisely the point: Circus Arts has no boundaries; be who you want to be, push your own skills, invent your art.

Invent your Art; invent yourself.

That would be my path.

Not particularly caring about the judgement of others, I tried everything there was. I fell in love with the aerial world. The coach had a muscle mass the likes of which I'd only seen on TV. He would lift me to the trapeze like I was a feather.

From that day on, art has never left my life. I had fallen in love with what would remain my loyal partner for the next few decades.

I had to convince my parents this would be my new purpose, that I had no intention of going back to gymnastics, and that I wanted to practice circus arts as often as possible. It may have seemed like a sudden and infatuated decision, especially coming from an 11-year-old. Still, my already well-honed conviction skills, and probably the sparkle in my eyes, made my mission successful. My parents accepted to make their full-time working lives even more complicated by now having to drive me to the big city for practice.

The only condition they had given me was that I—not them—had to tell my gymnastics coach that I wouldn't go back to what had been until now, my priority. It obviously insulted the coach who sarcastically wished me 'good luck' with my 'little clowning sessions'.

Years later, when I was regularly on international TV shows, she would self-promote as 'my former coach'.

THE CALL

A few months later, in February, Karine and I were already learning quite a lot on our aerial hoop, a big metal ring hung in the air used as a trapeze. It was not a popular apparatus back in 1994. We were partnering like pros. Our examples were the Steben twins. Karyne and Sarah Steben were identical twins partnering on the trapeze on the show Saltimbanco by a new, amazing company the world had started to talk about: Cirque du Soleil. Karine and I had seen them on TV; their skills were insane. The media claimed they had 'invisible magnets' in their feet—they could hold one another by only their feet whilst swinging in the air on the trapeze. We thought we'd do anything to perform on that level and a lot higher. We were fearless little girls wanting to conquer the world.

February 18, 1995, Sunday morning, 6:30 a.m., I jump out of bed to get ready for my day at the circus. On Sundays, we trained from 9 a.m. to 5 p.m. I am in the bathroom when the phone rings. I rush to the living room to pick up since the household is still sleeping. There is an odd voice asking to talk to my mom. Probably Karine's mother, but I did not recognise her, so I call my mother.

I went back to the bathroom to continue my girly preparation, and when I come out, my mom and dad are standing by the phone receiver. Mom is crying.

Karine wouldn't come with us that morning. In fact, she wouldn't come again. She had passed away the day before.

I show no visible emotions, but my legs give way under me, and I end up half seated on the couch. The pain is roaring inside my chest, leaving no space for breathing. A feeling I can't explain at the time, let alone process. That day, in the afternoon, I ask my parents to drive me to the circus. I only want one thing: to numb everything by doing what I like the most. The circumstances of such loss are impossible to endure to this day.

In her short life, Karine made the most significant difference in mine.

1.1

I don't believe in talent

_____

Being talented won't make you world-class;
decades of dedication will.

Talent is not a gift of God; it's earned. I'm sorry for bursting your bubble.

We heard numerous stories as the skinny boy bullied at school became the greatest fighter in mixed martial arts (MMA) history (think Georges St-Pierre). Apart from the fact that they sound good on TV, these stories aren't rare. In most fields, you face competition from the very beginning. In acting, as in circus arts, science, sports, and music, there will always be a child who seems genetically crafted for the purpose. I now believe, in most cases, this child won't make it to the top. Being perfect for the job makes it easy at the beginning, during the period where the learning curve is still steep. You rise fast and high; all eyes are on you. However, what counts is what comes after: *the decades of dedication.*

It takes 10% of your career and efforts to become great at something; the remaining 90% will be spent on becoming excellent, to belong to the elite. That 90% of time and effort may only represent a small improvement in skill, but it's what makes all the difference. That amount of energy, consistency, and patience will give you a slight chance at becoming world-class.

Becoming one of the very few is only possible through barely human daily consistent efforts—a level of dedication one has to master. A person who starts as 'a natural' might not work on their learning skills in a proper, possibly painful, way. When this person plateaus, the one with no foreseen 'talent' but real hunger will overtake the previously talented one and never stop rising at a steady pace, up to the moon.

Remember you may be the best in your village but still a drop in the ocean.

OBSTACLES AS TOOLS

A path without obstacles is not one that leads to success. Not because you got lucky but because you stayed in the no-obstacle zone, where people zigzag their way through mediocrity and never arrive anywhere meaningful.

Every story of elite performance gathers its level of unbelievable trouble.

Think of Wendy Whelan who, as a child ballerina, was told that her severe scoliosis gave her no chance of a ballet career. She became New York City Ballet's principal dancer for more than 15 years and inspired generations to come. Tommy Caldwell, the first person to free climb the Dawn Wall of Yosemite's El Capitan—the most difficult big wall free route in the world—an exploit that no one thought possible. Let alone he did it with only nine fingers; Tommy accidentally lost his index finger years before.

Obstacles are a filter; everyone faces them. Most people will decide that it's too hard and call it a day. A few will walk through the fire to get where they want to be. Those are the future elite performers of this world. There is a price to pay for not staying in the mass. The reward is outstanding.

On the other hand, obstacles—financial, genetic, circumstantial, especially when added to one another in a short amount of time—will eventually feel like a dead-end road. When there is always a fire to extinguish, it's difficult to remember why we carry on. It's sometimes almost a miracle to only take a step ahead towards our goal as we go through the day. For instance, rehabbing a recurrent injury, commuting for hours daily to get to the training studio, facing rejection innumerable times.

There are a few things to remember each time a rock destroys your perfectly paved road. First of all, the fire extinguishing time is also a learning opportunity. It sounds somewhat cliché but how true. Overcoming obstacles is a moment of improvement in disguise. You become more efficient at it. Although it feels like you are losing time for the primary goal, you are learning, gathering mental muscles, developing hunger. Once on the other side of the obstacle, you are already a step ahead of where you were before. It seems like you just ran in place and lost time, but in fact, you just got upgraded.

It's common to witness a famous ballerina or an elite athlete who is forced to be out of the spotlight for a long period of time (e.g. Svetlana Zakharova, Roger Federer). A period that would typically lead to the death of a career, only to come back stronger. When busy fighting obstacles—battling a grave sickness, bringing a child into the world—it is possible to keep improving your craft from a different angle.

When facing difficult situations, concentrate on the new inputs to learn from. You are handed a problem-solving opportunity on a silver platter. Switching your viewpoint may allow you to seize opportunities that were in a blind spot. It's not a waste of time. Instead, it's a chance to reprioritise and create a more efficient learning curve. It's also a test of persistence and a reminder not to take any day for granted; tomorrow could always be your last practice. The threat must become a motivator.

Obstacles popped up throughout my career. Life seems to have an unlimited supply of them; they are a renewable resource. Not only did I want to swim on my own, I wanted to fly, and I'd used every rock on the path to propel myself higher. When you are striving to get somewhere precise, your eyes are on the vision. You fuel yourself with the improvements, daily ones, as minuscule as they might seem.

DON'T GET TOO COMFORTABLE

The luckiest of us, born in first-world countries with no major health issues, can partially avoid obstacles by never taking risks and living with a lifebuoy. When you have a plan B to fall back on—be it wealthy parents who will help if your business fails or simply a too comfortable life to really make your goal a 'live or die' situation—you might not be equipped for what will inevitably come if you want to reach summits of a particular field. It takes strength to keep your head above water when difficulties keep dragging you down.

As a child, I liked the idea of the Soviet Union training style: gruelling efforts producing outstanding results. I had not understood the subtleties of smart planning, a good training programme, and sports psychology, but I was ready to be uncomfortable to reach my goals. In hindsight, ballet might have been too comfortable for me. I craved being pushed to high levels and instead I was being congratulated and pampered. I wanted to learn through discomfort, to raise my resilience and know I was stronger than any urge of giving up at any time. I needed to feel a sense of invincibility to failure if I wanted to achieve something meaningful. Finding something difficult means you are showed you must improve. And improving is one of my favourite things in the world. There are places where you don't have the luxury to think it's too hard. Because whenever it clearly becomes too difficult for you, you just lost your opportunity of having a shot at it. Complacency is a luxury, and it promotes laziness. You can't be both lazy and dedicated.

Chapter 2

Show me the passion

Don't expect to be hit by a passion
as a bolt of lightning.

PHOTOGRAPHY: LOUISE LEBLANC

I'd do anything to become the best in the world.

Would you?

Putting the around-the-clock work into a craft without a burning passion would be torture. Would you willingly torture yourself with no decent motivation to do so? Your ability to commit to gruelling work to become the best all comes down to the intensity of your passion.

Are you motivated by intrinsic or extrinsic reasons? That alone will change not only the course of success and your ability to be truly committed but the very meaning of years of practice and eventually, years of life. Some are driven by the benefits that come with winning or by other people's dreams, and they sadly notice only decades later.

Would you choose the same path if there was only you to please?

When I started to compete internationally at the age of 14, I faced a new reality. Some of my rivals would continue to perform under the worst circumstances possible. On a broken leg, skin so consumed by a trapeze bar, you could almost see the inside tissues. I was impressed by their level of commitment for their art or what I romantically thought it was at the time. Nothing could stop them; they wanted to win at all costs, literally.

At the time, in some countries, artists received very little academic education aside from their sports/art. From a very early age, they only trained and barely learned to live in the real world. They were raised in their training academy; they saw their family twice a year. They were disconnected from the world and did not even know the basics of life. If they won international competitions, they had chances of a livelihood, and the state would help them financially when they'd retire from this short-lived career. If not, they'd go back to their country and have no future but to work in a factory in poor conditions for the rest of their life. That's when you MUST be the best. Although I do not encourage this path, it's a way to become world-class. The level of commitment when you have everything to lose in not reaching your goal makes you extremely good at your job. You absolutely need to be the best in the world, at all costs.

Being committed out of fear is a sad reality, and it's only sustainable for so long. The lack of intrinsic motivation eventually catches up. These talents usually decline fast, and the rest of the story is never pretty.

I prefer the alternative: when you have a purpose to fulfil for positive and personal reasons.

The desire to succeed will be intense. If you fail, your ego may be hurt, you'll have a little inner crisis, self-doubting (which can be rather painful), and you'll move on. But you will always move in the same direction. The motivation feeds you daily and hopefully forever.

All you want, all you see, is the ultimate goal. The will to attain it is so strong that nothing else ever reaches this level of importance. It becomes a life mission. Failing is as painful as for the ones who would lose everything because this goal is *your* everything. You can fall and get up countless times. Regardless of the results, your inner motivation is genuine.

HOW TO FIND YOUR PASSION

Don't expect to be hit by a passion as a bolt of lightning.

Passion does not instantly become such. As with love, the first infatuation might be powerful, but when difficulties arise, not only your determination and commitment but the time and energy you put into it will give it its true meaning. It will sharpen the desire and raise its value to your eyes.

Are you ready to go through hell for it? Do you have the courage to lead the life needed to reach the highest levels? If so, let's think about calling it a passion. Otherwise, you have a hobby. Don't put dirt on the word 'passion'.

One passion, if we ever craft one, is not practical; it's essential. Like the cure of a disease, water, or air.

I had no idea when I fell in love with circus arts at 11 years old what the ultimate goal would become. My dream was limited to a need to be the best from what I knew existed at the time. First, I dreamed of being chosen to participate in the Quebec Day summer show. Soon I visualised winning an international competition, of performing as a soloist during a world-famous opening. Eventually, I wanted to achieve a movement I had only seen men do at that point—to be the first in the world. Now it seems irrelevant, but these goals played a major role in the outcome. Had I not had these targets along the way, the effort wouldn't have sufficed to bring me to the level I reached today.

My references were the Festival de Cirque de Demain in Paris, where I could see the grace and perfection of the Moscow State Circus artists. I desperately wanted to move to Moscow as soon as I was of legal age to pursue my artistic education. To me, they were the best, and they looked better than everyone else featured in the competition. It was broadcast on television around the globe and featured artists from all continents, only the very best in their disciplines. I had to one day compete there.

At the Festival International du Cirque de Monte-Carlo, the stunts were death-defying. There was nothing of a higher level, acrobatically. The velvet voice of the master of ceremonies underlining acrobatic skills and a few vanity details made each of them unique. I did end up being invited to these two international events, achieving those targets as a soloist in 2007 and 2012. But, by that time, even if I was happy to take part in them, my goals had already evolved to the next level. I was dreaming of things more adapted to the person I had become. It did not make the previous points of reference irrelevant. Every one of these mini-goals served an important purpose on my road. They gave me direction, but they had to be transitory: goals have to continuously be created. Sometimes they appear disjointed as we change so much in a given time, but each one has its function to push you towards something more significant. Stagnation is the murderer of passions.

Only now I understand that a huge part of my passion is wanting to push my craft to unprecedented levels, running after perfection. Being in love with the end idea—the results—can be misleading. Most of your time will be spent in the pursuit of the dream and not in *living the dream*. A passion must englobe the process.

Your dreams will be crushed numerous times; your passion won't.

Find your interest. Explore it, sweat over it, make love to it, get angry at it. And if the desire remains unchanged, perhaps you may start to consider it a passion. There is a responsibility in naming it such. You must first give birth to it. When not feeding that desire becomes more painful than any risk or downside of pursuing it, when it burns inside, when your heartbeat speeds up every time you think of it, that's when the real passion manifests.

Beginning an international career

Fame is a dangerous poison.
Don't ever trade your passion for glory.

Cirque du Soleil was becoming more and more popular. They were to open shows in Las Vegas and were constantly featured on the international news, becoming a national pride in Canada. For my 11-year-old self, that was becoming something to look up to. Unaware that I would create a much broader vision and future for myself.

My first meaningful opportunities started to blossom at the age of 13. I flew to Toronto for the launch of Global TV at the Joker Nightclub with my 15-year-old colleague. We travelled in business class, and a limousine was waiting for us at the airport. They treated us like movie stars. We felt undeserving, probably rightly so. That night onstage, we wore different costumes than our usual, with the logo of the brand we were inaugurating. Our manager gave it to us before the show, and never suggested we try it 'in action' before we went on. For any acrobatic act, especially an aerial act, it is imperative to eliminate any additional risk factor by rehearsing with the costume for days if not weeks before the event. Just like a runner doesn't try new shoes the day of the marathon.

The music of Vangelis resonates through the venue as we fly dangerously close to the crowd. We hold the hoop and each other in precarious but graceful positions in the air. People have never seen such abilities at the time. Everyone is in awe. The costume is particularly slippery, so holding the metal hoop with various parts of our bodies requires much more strength. Towards the end of our performance, I usually cascade down the aerial hoop and slide onto my partner until we 'miraculously'—a word involving hours of practice—hook onto each other. She grips the bar with only her legs while I fasten mine on her upper body, both of us upside down. When the audience thinks that's the climax, we surprise them with another trick where my partner catches my one ankle at the very last second, and I bring the other foot to my head in a beautiful contortion. We performed this grand finale many times. It was my favourite moment of the act as it creates a nanosecond of fear and a loud reaction of the audience. This time, however, I slide right to the floor. A two-metre free fall, ending on my back on a hard floor. My partner's hands gesturing ferociously in the air as if they could still catch me. I lose my breath for a few seconds, I get up, I smile, and I finish the act as if nothing had happened.

That was the first fall of my career. There have been many since; the psychological ones being the most hurtful.

THE FEW BIG WINS AND THE FADING SIDE OF IT

A few months later, I was flying to Europe to perform at my first international competition in La Piste aux Espoirs in Belgium. It was the most exotic place I'd heard of at that time. The international panel of judges gave us the gold medal, and we also won the public award. I was competing against many different nationalities. They called us 'les petites Canadiennes' (the tiny Canadians). That was the first time I witnessed how hard the Chinese worked. It made me feel like a spoiled and lazy child.

When we returned to Canada, we were greeted by the whole circus school as well as our colleagues from the company and our families. The next day, we had interviews on primetime TV. There it was, my 15 minutes of fame. Back in Belgium, a reporter interviewing us had asked me how it felt to be there that day, the day that would mark the beginning of an important international career for such a young lady. I thought he embellished the reality a little. I had become the star of the village but noticed I was a peon in the international show business.

Fame is as short as the length of your performance; it does not give you genuine value. The next week, it was back to business as usual: school, training relentlessly, always unhappy with my daily results. This achievement would be written on a CV someday. There was one more trophy by the medals displayed in my bedroom. I came back from Europe with a few business cards I kept for years, but overall, it hadn't changed anything. No awards provide a shortcut for accomplishments. It's simply a little tap on the back to keep going in difficult times. This art, like dance or any elite sport, resets to zero every morning; the currency is counted in hours of deliberate practice. Perhaps my unconscious mind was already devouring this concept of consistency. I started training more and with more focus. I had seen more possibilities, hence more work. I had to free up time in my schedule.

A few months later, my partner and I were invited to a three-day skills test at the new headquarters of Cirque du Soleil in Montreal. This is basically a fancy word for a semi-private audition. Our manager had told us we were being looked at for a new show that was to open in Las Vegas. I was the youngest in the impressive studio that day. The whole picture was daunting; everyone looked at us when we entered the gigantic room. A spectacularly fit woman in a black unitard came to greet us. I was so nervous that I automatically reached for her wrist instead of the hand she was presenting me. Robotically, I did what I was trained to do: catch the wrist of my partner. My discomfort was growing into shame.

That day, coaches and choreographers I had heard of or seen on TV were to teach me. André Simard would look at us in the air, this very person who developed and promoted the acrobatic silk in the nineties. I was intimidated for the first 10 seconds each time, and then I'd do what I was asked. I was confident in my acrobatic and aerial skills; the most challenging had been the dance and interpretation class. I was too new in my 15-year-old body to be able to interpret concepts or feelings with only my body. Like a proper little humanoid, I had learned by repetition. I was a good acrobatic technician; I wasn't an artist. I hadn't learned to translate emotions into movements. At the time, I had no interest in such an exercise. I saw it as a waste of time. It took me probably another decade to understand fully the power of interpretation, both for myself and my audience, and another decade to acquire subtleties through it.

An audience can't spot the reason a performer is unique. Why they are moved to their core, and they won't ever forget this single person. They think it is perfection striking, but it's that special weapon: *interpretation*. It gives the audience the key to the emotional space of a performance. We have to learn to convey feelings through our Art without making it obvious, and this may take decades to master, if one ever does.

Our manager told us it was a done deal. We told our families, school and social circles we were leaving with Cirque du Soleil. My mother developed a skin condition out of the anxiety of losing her little girl to the world of show business. We nervously awaited final confirmations for weeks whilst I was projecting myself in my future life. We never left for Las Vegas as our ages would require special assistance, schooling, tutors, nannies—especially in the Sin City—which Cirque du Soleil was trying to avoid. We were not good candidates for them.

My dream was crushed into pieces.

Soon after, I signed my first real contract with a professional contemporary circus company that was born from Quebec City: Cirque Eos. I received a salary to do what I liked the most. I was the youngest girl of the 24 members of the show but fearless in my will to rise, to be featured in every act the company would create. From the age of 15 to 17, I trained with the circus school to fulfil academic requirements on top of the company practice hours full-time. I spent every second of free time training or thinking about techniques, drawing forms of interesting movements, interpreting new pieces of music. Until then, I had specialised in aerial arts, but that would change. I became acrobatically very competent, and my strength developed at the same pace as the efforts I was putting into my craft. My motivation was borderline obsessive, and fear didn't exist. Everything was possible, and if not, I'd make it so.

2.2

Own your failures, deserve your successes

They are a mirror of your daily choices.

I was still going to regular school at the time, with the slow pace of education it implies. Some teachers permitted me to do my homework for the upcoming days during their class, as long as I did not disturb anyone and kept my scores above 90%. I could learn faster and finish within a few hours instead of a whole day.

School—or the fact I had to attend it—was becoming an issue for me. I had begun to travel more and more, and the rehearsals for the company would often take place during school time. I had to ask for special permissions all the time, and now the approbation requests were becoming more critical. Yearly academic exams were looming. I'd have to postpone them for a Middle and South American tour that I had on my schedule.

My convincing skills improved a lot that year, spending time explaining first to my parents and then to everyone involved in the education system—teachers, school director—why I needed their support. I was explaining from scratch every time the work, the passion, the impossibility of missing a particular show for an exam, making them seize the negative impact it would have on my career. I made them feel attached to my Art, showing pictures and videos and ultimately, giving them a role to play in my dreams.

The following year I moved into a sport-art accelerated program at a school named Cardinal-Roy. There I could go to school only in the mornings and have the rest of the day to dedicate to my Art. They were more flexible on catching up missed exams and arranging tests, even in foreign countries. Students needed to keep their academic grade average above 80% to stay in the program.

Between the ages of 14 and 18, I don't remember even watching a movie to the end. My time was so well distributed to become a better artist; I had next to no free time. My time management skills were sharpening. When not on tour with the circus, I consumed most meals during my commute, so I did not have to stop to eat.

The show business world was often not suitable for my young age. Sins and excess were everywhere but never a temptation for me. I was only interested in improving my craft. I avoided anything that wasn't in line with the path of success I had traced. Self-control and willpower were very deeply engrained in me.

While colleagues and friends were partying after a show or only going out to eat, I was studying for my next exam or going to bed early so I could train before everyone else the next day. I was thoroughly organised, understanding it would make me more efficient and get me closer to my goals, faster. There was no space for unpredictability. I would study for high school on my flights or during airport waiting times. I could clearly determine whether something would help my mission or wouldn't.

My special situation had allowed me to go through a more condensed academic life, and I even attended university earlier. It gave me the chance to develop and use my autodidact side to the fullest.

They did not treat me as a child in this company. I learned to have my own back, to be responsible for my failures, to protect my interests, to defend myself when I was psychologically attacked. It killed a part of my childlike naivety, and I am grateful for it. I was born and raised in such a loving and protective family; harmful human beings were not a processed concept to me. Through this life experience and the accelerated introduction to adulthood, I received a crash course on life. As a consequence, I learned to own my successes and know what it had taken me to get to where I was, leaving no space for any ill-intentioned people around me in the future. And there would be a few.

I also noticed quickly that those in positions of power would tend to want to own my success, although they had little to do with it, but suddenly deny all responsibility when something bad happened.

Human nature?

For a teenager moving into her young adult years, I already had decent self-esteem. My character was being forged solidly through every single failure. Every time I wasn't chosen for a role I had dreamed of, worked for, and thought I deserved more than anyone else, I was acquiring the strength I'd need later on for tougher experiences. Little by little, with curable psychological scars, I was becoming unbreakable, or at least I felt so.

My successes and failures are mine entirely to this day. They are consequences of my daily choices. Realising that we have our lives in our own hands is the first and most important step towards success. Freedom. Empowerment.

EFFORTFUL AND ORGANISED LEARNING

Tiny details, repeated with consistency, will change the course of events. The extra effort at the end of a daily six-hour training session won't pay off after a few weeks, but with years, it might draw the gap that will make you number one worldwide. With micro-changes to my days, training, and habits, although they appeared insubstantial, I'd see improvements. And they became exponential.

I soon grew addicted to pushing my boundaries to find out what the results would be. The fine-tuning process of my life and Art, from a daily consideration, turned into an intrinsic habit.

Some say I had no childhood.

I did have a childhood: travelling around the world, learning new cultures, improving a craft that became an identity while forging a solid career, meeting exceptional human beings, learning languages, acquiring life skills such as discipline, humility, responsibility.

It's been a matter of conscious choice, fed by a burning fire. I wanted to stand out of the mass by raising the bar. In the process, I raised the expectations I held for myself. No one ever pushed me. If anything, my beloved ones, instead, had the unsuccessful habit of trying to slow me down.

I *did* have a childhood and quite an extraordinary one.

JEALOUSY: WHEN YOU GET NOTICED

The concept of jealousy has had its secondary role throughout the movie of my life. I never had the time, energy, or will to feed it. I was busy aiming for more, getting better. I remember hearing my colleagues not so subtly gossiping on the rehearsal floor under me whilst I was five metres above them in the air, practising.

'She has a soloist role because she is slimmer'. 'The head coach likes her better'.

'… unfair …'

'… do with it …'

I was training and performing with these women. They danced on the floor and moved the long pieces of fabric I was tying myself onto, nine metres up in the air. There was a sense of sisterhood when we travelled or went out after a training session, but the reality was that me being a soloist was taking that spot away from another, and tension arose from it. Some of them trained harder and became fairly successful later on, but the ones gossiping behind my back remained gossipers.

One day, there was a special meeting with all the artists and the management of the company. One topic was me having too many parts in the show. My counterparts argued that it was unfair; I was benefiting too much, being seen on stage too much. Someone else would be pleased with this or that role. My talent or skills were never in question, nor my commitment or hard-working personality. The directors would politely listen and say they'd consider what had been said. In the end, competence drove the decisions. No company leader would willingly choose the employee who is not the best at the task. And while some were busy being jealous and plotting some sort of master plan to remove me from my position, I was busy creating an even greater distance between me and them. The time I would have lost defending myself and making things right in this unfair attack, I used instead to prove my point: I was better then, and now even more.

As a 16-year-old with all the insecurities and doubts that age carries, in front of women I should have looked up to, I demanded social and moral validity. And I was admittedly a little intimidated. But not for long. I became aware of the uselessness of being liked by everyone. The higher I'd climb in the hierarchy—for the right reasons—the more I'd upgrade my skills, the more I'd disturb, the more I'd face people claiming the unfairness of the situation. My answer? Impermeability.

Chapter 3

Come to my room little girl

The unembellished realities of show business.

In the early summer days, the company left for Europe again for an artistic project that seemed of the highest importance. All the directors and choreographers who rarely travelled with the cast were present on this occasion. I was one of the youngest girls in the cast again and quite noticeable. Not only because I was the protagonist of many performances in the show but because I still physically looked almost like a child. I did not hang out much with the group; when not practising on my own, I liked to watch the choreographer work with other artists. I was absorbing. One could certainly notice I was striving for perfection. I arrived early to warm up and verify everything before rehearsals, even if that meant going with the technical team transport instead of the artistic bus. I was frequently the last to leave after rehearsals, still correcting what had gone unperfected in my performances.

The program was impressive; it took place in a huge, staged flowery garden behind a castle. After the first days of practice, the entire cast and technical team felt like characters from *Alice in Wonderland*. It was magnificent. I was proud to perform, knowing the well-lit organic background of nature enhanced my show. I performed in many different spots of the royal garden. In one scene, my aerial silks were rigged to an enormous centenarian tree. A professional technician and engineer lifted me, pulling on the carefully installed ropes. During the rehearsal, he made a mistake in the timing and pulled me up earlier than agreed. My thumb remained stuck in an odd position, resulting in a sprain. It turned blue and swollen. That wouldn't stop me from performing the next day, but I spent months working in pain because of this small accident.

People were amazed by my parts in the show; compliments were flowing in my direction. The director and choreographers congratulated me after each of my appearances. It had only been the dress rehearsals, but the show was promising. The excitement was tangible. That night, we were notified that there was a little gathering in a room of the castle before the cast and crew would be driven to their dormitories. The travelling conditions were far from luxurious at the time; dorms with shared bathrooms were not an exception.

The local producer of the event had seen the practices that night. Everyone was a little intimidated by the big boss witnessing them at work. We all wished he had seen us at our best. I was no exception; I wanted to impress. After dinner, people were having drinks, and most artists were going back to the dormitory already. I did not drink. The fact that I was underage did not really matter to anyone, but I just did not see how alcohol would ever serve any purpose for me.

The producer came personally to congratulate me. I was ecstatic.

This man was three or four times my age, but I was used to handling conversations with adults. After exchanging a few trivialities—the weather and Belgian chocolate—I said I had to go back to the dormitories.

'Aren't you staying in a nice hotel nearby?' he asked.

'No sir, we are staying in school residences'. I surely did not want to sound like I was complaining. My company director was standing about a metre behind Mr Producer, unnoticed. He could probably hear our conversation, and I was afraid he'd misinterpret it.

'You deserve better; you are our star'.

I noticed all my colleagues had left already, and for a minute, I feared I had missed the artistic shuttle. But I saw the head coach of the company from afar verifying if anyone was left. He noticed me and gestured me to come.

'Wait a second!' said the producer, posing his hand behind my neck. He got closer to my ear so he could lower his voice: 'I'll organise a room for you so you can have a hot bath and have a proper rest. We will take care of your hand'.

He had noticed I was applying ice on the injured part and inquired about it. Flattering words, kind offer. My heartbeat was accelerating.

Despite his insistence, I politely declined and left.

Later on at the dormitory, my company director wanted to meet me. He said I was stubborn and had done something impolite. This was one of our big clients, he reminded me.

'Has your mom never taught you how to behave with important people?' he asked. I looked him in the eyes, stayed silent, and classified him in my head.

I slept in my uncomfortable bed that night, after a cold shower. No one took care of my injury.

End of the story.

Now hearing about horrific children abuses in organisation where adults fail to protect them, I shiver. I feel tremendously lucky and a little hopeful that children won't have to grow used to refusing producers' advances and get blamed by those who should act as their protector.

Chapter 4

From passion to vision

The path to success is a battlefield,
not a fairy tale.

PHOTOGRAPHY: BOAZ ZIPPOR

'Choose a job you love, and you will never
have to work a day in your life'.
~ Confucius

I couldn't disagree more. Here is my updated version of that famous quote: Do what you love for a living, and you'll work as if your life depended on it. It will drive you crazy on a regular basis. You will not only have to endure, but you will have to thrive with a level of stress that would destroy most people. You'll invest everything you have, including your most precious currency: time. It will take up all the space in your life. People around you will blame you for being so obsessed with 'that vision'. It will be a 24/7, 365 days commitment each year. A renewed vow every single morning.

Signing that contract is a lifetime of dedication. You have to be ready to do something that might not work, but do it as if your life depends on it over and over again. The good news is that it might be worth every headache and drop of sweat.

The rare gratification I get out of looking at my work and liking it is priceless.

At 19 years old, I was a soloist in the contemporary circus company I worked for, travelling around the world, living the dream, receiving a decent salary for my age. I had social and financial security as well as my life ahead of me. But I was starving for more. I had this vision of creating my Art. I imagined far higher possibilities. I did not even know then that one could do such physical work in her/his adult years. I did not know what possible market there was away from circuses or theatres. I decided to quit the company nonetheless to work freelance and build my own brand. I didn't know the path to pursue. I was certainly not aiming to follow a role model; I had never had one. I knew that my possible market was international, but there was no map, no guidebook. I could create my *Physical Poetry* and make it world-famous—my form of Art, no one else's.

A passion should be regarded and treated as a privilege. The passion of a lifetime should be able to make up for losing friends, the most intense loneliness, the lack of sleep and social life, the constant physical discomfort, the incessant inflammation in your whole body, the lack of income, the taste of not being enough, not doing enough, not knowing enough. These feelings will haunt you, day and night.

Don't start pursuing something with the aim of being great. Pursue something because it is the most fascinating pursuit of your life, because you want to push it to an unprecedented level. Every single achievement should be a victory, but the bittersweet victory that only pushes you to want more.

Without a clear goal, however, that passion will remain a simple dream. The vision you'll create out of your passion needs to become so clear that even on the worst day in a decade—when you've been stagnating for months and you ache like never before, when you've been rejected for the 36th time this year—you never lose sight of your vision.

At that precise moment, make sure the intention is crystal clear. Write in detail exactly what you want to achieve, how it will taste, how it will look, how you will feel when you reach that ultimate goal, how you will emotionally react to the numerous failures along the way. Use the answers as a compass. Make that vision so clear and detailed that it becomes ingrained in you. It's what you see when you first wake up in the morning; it's what's on your mind when you are lost in thought driving in traffic.

You need to be obsessed with this vision because unless you are, you won't be able to bear what is required to get there. You'll have to learn every single facet, attribute, and downside of that notion. You'll know so much of your craft that every hair-thin speck of dust is perceivable only to you. It becomes your life's mission. You'll have such a profound faith in it that it is unshakeable. You'll face an immense amount of dissuasion—from your loved ones, from society—but the worst will come from yourself.

At 19, I did not know what I'd need to invest to achieve what I had in mind. I had the vision of being worldwide famous for performing my own Art, but single goals were still to be defined and a master plan to design.

DON'T FOLLOW THE PATH, CREATE IT.

I wasn't aware of a possible gap in the market for my project to fill, and if there had been one, I don't believe it would have changed my path. I was going to build the road to my success, to create the need and not the other way around. The recurrent question I'd receive was: 'Where will you work? In which circus? Theatre? Dinner show?'

I did not have a clear answer because it did not matter. What mattered was creating a craft so powerful that it would break all the walls of that given market. My Art would speak for itself.

I knew what I wanted, but I had to create a system that would allow me to make that vision a reality. A system that still to this day, I keep fine-tuning, adding the slightest improvement every single day: the plan of my success.

There is no guidebook other than the one you are designing.

The road to the most important stages around the world is long to build and very bumpy. Make mistakes, but each of them only once. And with new mistakes, make sure to find new solutions instead of finding comfort in the known ones. A burning will, not fear, should lead the way.

The follower always remains behind. Stop wanting to be as good as the industry leader, surpass the masters, or compete with anyone. The target is misplaced. Instead, focus that energy on your craft. Be so focused on details, no one should be able to read the map of success you used.

Chapter 5

The master plan

Discipline is freedom; consistency is key.

The extrinsic attributes of my life are very chaotic: living geographically everywhere and nowhere, frequently performing in three different countries in a single week, literally living in hotel rooms around the world, three meals a day in restaurants, the irregularity of a freelance worker's income— bringing loads of work all at the same time and then gaps of emptiness—ever-changing schedules, making it challenging to stick to a repetitive program needed as an athlete. As if all of this was not tumultuous enough, the very nature of showbusiness is known better for its distraction and unpredictability than its rigour and accuracy.

Do any of these attributes qualify for reasons not to behave in the exact way I should to reach my goals? Certainly not!

I have to live the life of a monk; numerous hours of training each day, a strict and monotonous diet, healthy sleeping habits, planned creative sessions at specific moments during my waking hours. I have to be at my prime every single day of the year as there is no off season for me, no holidays. The biggest opportunity of my life may be just around the corner. I can't afford to not be at the top on a given day. I can't afford a cold, let alone the flu, or an extra few grams of fat on my body.

Living, training, and performing at this cadence, I had to forge a solid discipline to keep up with the requirements. Not only to sustain that lifestyle but to continue to improve as an athlete, a businesswoman, and a human being. Most of my time and energy could have been consumed by only getting through this round-the-world type of schedule, but it wouldn't be sufficient to maintain the pace of an ever-changing showbusiness environment. That would translate into stagnation, and it is not an option. As a result, I have learned to use every single hour, flight, waiting moment, pre- and post-performance, as efficiently as possible to keep moving towards mastering my vision.

Consistency is the key to a highly inconsistent environment. Any interference distracts you from your goal, so your choices should be obvious.

Planning solidifies your discipline, and discipline is your freedom. By designing your plan down to the smallest detail, you leave little room for error and no chance for ultimate failure. Every morning, the only choice you will make to make your vision happen is to follow the plan you've crafted. A restrictive lifestyle means freedom since you automatise the not-so-pleasant tasks through singular habits. Then you have the remaining time to create, discover, improve, and indulge. With the same strategy through life, you can achieve anything. It's a cause and effect formula.

We like to make things complicated and pretend that complexity magically turns that very thing into something valuable. You shouldn't have time to make things complex; you should only have time to make things work. Systems at their purest state are most efficient. Fine-tune the system, following the constraints of the moment. No detail should be left random; everything you can use in your favour should become a trick to thrive further. Simple tricks become habits. Habits become inherent, and no extrinsic data should change any of this.

Never allow *excuses*—what some call *exceptions*—to not follow the plan: Christmas for overeating, jet lag for not sleeping enough, an achievement to celebrate instead of going to sleep at a toddler's bedtime. Each exception slows you down, and exceptions added to exceptions create mediocrity. The cost is too high.

Every downside of the life you've chosen should be part of the plan. Find a use for it; foresee it. Don't regard them as obstacles or random events to deal with when they show up; expect them.

They are solely elements to juggle, and each of them should have a pre-decided order of response. Be allergic to reasons not to succeed. Be repulsed by procrastination, even the very hidden type. Limitations, or the lack of, are self-created. You can divide the most difficult skills into easy-to-learn abilities you can practice repetitively to master.

While others are busy complaining about a situation, get busy correcting it or making the best of it. If the given case doesn't allow so, move away.

The equation is simple: what do you want and what are the tangible actions to make repetitively for a given amount of time/years to get there? Once that's defined, you can build the master plan.

5.1

Personality building

You can be your own worst enemy or best ally.

B uild a strong character, and you'll have the most powerful tool for life, either to build or sadly, to destroy. And this also applies towards yourself. Train your mind to respond accordingly to any stimulus. The more you rise in hierarchy or success, the more you'll need it. Amateur careers come with amateur problems. Be the best, and you'll get the most important problems: it's a free upgrade. Just be ready to face them.

Success comes with pressure, and I perceive this as a blessing. It's much more rewarding to stand out in a field where your competitors are all extraordinary. They contribute to making you better.

Many Olympic athletes plan their training schedule annually and up to four years in advance to make sure they'll reach their specific goal. A business will fix its growth goal and align accordingly. Why wouldn't we do that as individuals? There is a lack of self-importance and long-term planning when it comes to ourselves. Getting fit shouldn't be only about summer-swimsuit vanity but about the way you'll look and feel at 70, 85, 99 years old. You are deciding the very quality of your life for the decades to come and yet focussed merely on next summer. Every daily action will influence the outcome and should be taken seriously. You owe your future full self-honesty. Investigate your motivations. Are they shallow or deep? Do you romantically want a certain outcome (i.e. bikini body for vanity) filtering out what it implies? Or do you have the genuine will—full commitment—not to bail out of the process until you incarnate what you really want? That includes days or years of repetitive choices. Don't make the mistake to desire an outcome but disregard the process it implies and act surprised when reality hits.

Make daily plans for life achievements. With that mindset, I train and keep improving daily. In my relatively short performer's career, the daily efforts I consistently put into my craft for 15 years made me world-famous in my twenties. And although I won't pretend any of this was easy, I committed to the process long before it became real.

It's crucial to be coherent in daily choices and actions: you want elite results; you have to forge an elite personality.

DELAY GRATIFICATION

Gratification is overrated. Think of it as a shiny object: once in the dark, it loses its appeal. Maybe we are just unable to foresee things in a different light when they stand in front of us?

Rationally speaking, anyone would resist the temptation of an immediate, shiny reward (unhealthy food, staying in bed) in preference of a later reward that might change your life for the better. Sins providing immediate rewards shouldn't sound appealing if you do that simple math. And yet we keep committing actions that are opposed to our direction. Why?

If you fail continuously at refusing instant gratification that will delay the achievement of a goal, it might be time to think about a replacement gratification. Link a pleasant reward to making the right choice and an unpleasant response to giving into a bad habit. Personally speaking, the very act of having made the right choice for my utmost goal *is* the instant gratification. If that's not your case; you might use tricks to choose the most unpleasant steps until they become automatic. Waking up at 5 a.m. for a run will be torture the first few weeks until it becomes a pleasant time of introspection and your body asks for the blood flows it delivers. You will eventually link that behaviour to a sense of pride. As silly as this may sound, it works. We adapt to what we submit ourselves to. That's the exact system I use continuously to do what's right for me in the long run, but complete torture in the moment of doing it. I consciously learned to disregard the painful part.

There is no connection with the 'no pain, no gain' motto, which I consider outdated. To be clear: that is not courage, it's nonsense. There is no point in going through unnecessary pain: if pain can be avoided and the result is attained with same efficiency, choose the pain-free option, no question. But most meaningful achievements imply difficult actions to get there, hence unpleasant repeated steps. It is possible to interpret unpleasant experiences in another way, even to trick yourself into craving that very action. We would all benefit from upgrading what we see as challenging to a few steps higher on the difficulty scale. Average has never been a very glamourous attribute.

Every single habit serving your mission must be as established in your daily routine as brushing your teeth. By regularly prac-tising something challenging, you'll improve many of your skills; Deepening skills can be transferred to other fields, and that's when the improvements become exponentials.

Don't be content unless you become what you wanted, not the bargaining version of it. Contentment is the beginning of the end. You don't have to lower your standards and the quality of your dreams because others do. It's fine to remain out of the mass. Do you want to be ordinary? Or do you want to acquire a personality that will let you accomplish genius exploits over and over again? Aim to be your own role model. After all, self-worth represents the reputation you have with yourself.

SELF-WORTH AND VALIDATION

When I became a freelance artist, I knew I needed to develop my entrepreneurial side and make myself visible to the world. Instead of auditioning for every artistic opportunity that was dangling out there, I enrolled in the Chamber of Commerce of Quebec City. I immediately signed up for the first networking event. At 6 a.m., motivated business people, mostly middle-aged men, met up in a trendy restaurant to have breakfast together and pitch their new idea or brag about their last success. I woke up at 4:45 a.m. that day, dressed as a grown-up, and drove to the city where the meeting was taking place. I had just left the company I had toured the world with for years, which means I didn't have an apartment yet. I was temporarily living in my parents' basement in the suburbs, kilometres from the city.

I arrive at the restaurant, leave my winter jacket at the entrance, and walk towards the sign designing the area for the Entrepreneurs. The hostess immediately points out that I am in the wrong area of the restaurant: 'This one is reserved for Chamber of Commerce members', she naggingly exclaims.

I tell her my name is on the list.

Not even feeling ashamed for not letting me talk initially, she opens the gate she so carefully guarded.

When I start connecting with other members, before we eventually sit at our respective tables, I am asked twice where my parents are. A man engages in a flirty conversation. What a crowd!

Whilst coffee is being served, elevator pitch time comes. I am very comfortable explaining my international background and future ideas. Why I became a freelancer and how I am going to build international awareness. Other members are barely listening, some chatting in between, not to miss the person with deep pockets I assume. I am sharp, ambitious, realistic, and have probably worked in more countries than all of the seven other men seated with me combined. But that is not sufficient for them to pay attention. One of them eventually suggests that I work for Cirque du Soleil, earning the 'smart comment award' of the day from his peers.

I thought it wouldn't be long before I'd make them swallow their words.

Two years later, at the yearly distinction awards thrown by the same Chamber of Commerce, I won, together with my stage partner, the prize for international distinction for our work and business. I don't know if any of the men who had a good time not taking me seriously that morning were amongst the crowd; I had forgotten their face long ago. They certainly did not belong in my league.

By raising your standards towards yourself, you'll realise that there are not many things you can categorise as problematic. Everyone has past trauma to excuse what they haven't accomplished. Ditch yours, learn to hate self-pity, and stop lying to yourself. You are not that special, not that unique. Take full responsibility for your successes and failures.

Mental strength is a skill to train; some call it talent.

Building the plan

Skip steps and limp forever.

There is a perfect formula in every process. It's worth putting the necessary time to sharpen the learning abilities for any given skill. Consider this process at the beginning of anything you want to learn or achieve essential. Become a methodology expert at your craft and learn faster.

Where to start?

Are your goals and priorities working in the same direction? Sometimes the priority isn't serving the long-term goal but needs to be rectified, nonetheless. By priority, I don't mean the void reasons that serve a procrastination purpose, but the very actions that, without achieving, won't let you move forward with your goal. For instance, if I have an injury to address, and I must postpone the six-month training plan designed to acquire new skills for a given event. The medium-term results I had in mind suffers, but it's the priority. By leaving it unaddressed, you'll continuously be back to square zero. To define priority, you must have a global and long-term picture: a vision.

Second, allow time and energy to build an uncompromising foundation: the basics. It's easy and quite accessible to skip steps, to want to flirt with the highest skills without having learned the basics of a craft. It's wiser to spend the number of years necessary to become as solid as possible with the fundamentals of your art. You will need them later, and there won't be time to go back to them once your career is going full steam. The unlearning process to re-learn properly is extremely psychologically painful. The classical roots of a musician or dancer will inevitably give them tools to reach the highest level of their art, although not limited to classical. It will also allow them to master any variety of their field more quickly. Cheat the learning process, and you'll have to deal with the missing part of the puzzle later. I think of it as consciously choosing to limp forever for the trade of a shortcut.

I'm not a patient person, but I had to change this feature of my personality to learn in the proper order. I am thankful I did. For learning a new language or a new movement of my *Physical Poetry*, understanding the roots of anything increase the future potential of reaching high levels. Skipping steps isn't efficient; it is stupid.

Designing the master plan, consider three spheres: short-, medium, and long-term plans. Although counter-intuitive, the most important to address and be consistent with is the short-term plan. Be diligent in designing your daily life; it is the mirror of your entire project. Don't leave anything random. Once you take the time to design it—each detail should be linked to logical foreseen outcomes—stick to that plan without exception.

Set the stage for success. Whatever is lacking in your personality, compensate for it in the plan, until you acquire it.

Do not rely entirely on your willpower just yet. To help you make the right choices every single day, make the first step of each desired habit as automatic as possible, by making them easy to initiate. For years, on my nightstand with my passport, I'd lay out my sports clothes ready to do my 90-minute cardio and body awakening before taking a taxi to the airport for the next transcontinental flight. That often meant waking up at 3:10 a.m. instead of 5 a.m. Since I was flying abroad often four to six times a week, it was the best system I had found to make sure I had enough cardio training in my schedule. Whatever the goal is, help yourself make the right decisions. Every decision brings you closer to your future self, the one who attains the vision. Especially at the beginning of a plan, when habits are not yet ingrained. Do not leave space for doubt; provide yourself with no chance to fail at the project.

Through systems and habit creating, I became a master at enduring hardship because I know the outcomes it creates. I know it is a necessary part of the process; it serves my vision. I've learned to enjoy a sense of physical exhaustion, and unless I reach it every single day, I'm not satisfied with myself. No instant gratification—what people call *enjoying life*—is worth my attention. My mission is clear, and whatever I do successfully to get closer to it creates joy.

The medium-term plan, set at six months for me, is there to create a sense of deadline. I see it as a motivator and timeframe to keep me in check with my aspirations. If I follow the daily plan, in six months, I should have lost a given amount of body fat, acquired this new movement I am working on, finished this artistic piece, or automated my online promotion tool. If that is not the case, I adapt the daily plan with all the data I have.

Do not chop and change your plan continuously to adapt to daily noise. Take these realities into account when building the daily program: days are messy. Do reassess and make changes, but at intervals of six months (medium-term) rather than day-to-day. Hence the importance of thinking the short-term plan through thoroughly. You'll inevitably have ups and downs during this medium-term window. If you keep adapting the daily plan, you only respond to what is happening daily. Following temporary stimuli, which include emotional responses to new challenges, would be a terrible way to zigzag your way towards your goal. Stick to the plan and adapt it to medium-term threshold only.

The longer-term is your utmost vision; it is the very reason *why*—the big picture. It all starts by making this one as clear and vivid as possible.

Testing the boundaries

The fake 'freedom' of unstructured people.

PHOTOGRAPHY: BOAZ ZIPPOR

That week, I had given myself a bit more freedom in my work, choosing not to have a precise plan as I normally do. Maybe what others assumed was 'exaggerated rigidity' was really keeping me away from a world of greatness.

The evening prior to a new week, I pause and write all my weekly intentions on paper. It's a very beautiful, almost meditative ritual I created many years ago, not only on the eve of a new week but to start any new chapter of my life with clear purposes and a structured method. I use the term structured as it is not impermeable to changes. It can be adapted to suit the ever-changing needs of the environment you are working in. Being conscious of that, I try to remain open and alert, within a certain range, to modify the road I had previously decided to take. I call it my schedule-plasticity.

I am a 'professional list maker' as well as a borderline control freak. Not taking this precious time to structure my week and visualise where I wanted to be at the end of this time-lapse was my first big mistake. I am usually thrilled looking at a new blank page of opportunities, anything new, from moving to a new continent to starting a big creation for a precise project or just undertaking a new week. This time, I felt a bit lost, and my usual energy towards anything challenging was absent. That alone put me in a state of anxiety.

DAY ONE:
Day one started as usual but with a frustrating lack of efficiency. I felt overwhelmed by everything there was to do. I knew what time I was going to practice but not having fixed more than this, the rest of my day lacked focus. Typically, day one is my strongest day for training; body and mind are rested. This time, I found myself trying to work with a limited body. Looking back, I'm quite sure

my physical condition was in a perfect state and could have been a great tool to do wonders, but my mind shut it down and was convincing enough to make it blind to its usual capacities. I was tired and not very strong. I cut my training short by 30 minutes and went home without any sense of accomplishment that night.

DAY TWO:

The next morning, I set my alarm clock a little bit later than usual, woke up sluggish, and felt tired with no trace of motivation to be found.

Throughout the years, I have developed many tricks to find the motivation or fire I need when it's not coming easily. I have a series of exercises and questions to go through if needed, but normally, just sticking to my day plan is enough to get me started. By doing so, I create a flow, and the energy starts manifesting again. Nothing seemed to work this time; I lacked a sense of purpose. I felt so unenergised that maybe it was a signal that something was wrong, and I should take a day off from training to concentrate on other areas of work and life. I listened to what I thought was an early sign of exhaustion. A decision I later regretted as I could not rationalise it. I felt guilty and lazy to sacrifice a precious day of training. And day two ended more lost than it had started.

DAY THREE:

I woke up in a much better state and started with many projects in the early hours. When the time came for my first training session, I became whiny, and instead of starting with energy and power, I went through training like someone was forcing me to do so. A slight sense of satisfaction hit me afterwards, but when the second and more intense practice session came, I hit a psychological wall, and many thoughts I wouldn't even dare to share bombarded my mind. I managed to ignore them. Once in my training studio, I sat unenthusiastically; I couldn't even find the energy to put on my training clothes and start a three-hour session. Consumed by the lack of structure, I noticed that I produced no creative work that week. I thought I had the proof there was something wrong with me.

Here I am on day three of what should be an amazing week of achievements, learning the lesson that my call-it-crazy-if-you-want habit of planning, structuring, calculating, list-making, and foreseeing everything is not working against creativity but actually allowing it. This little experiment had been motivated by a desire to be more imaginative in my schedule, breaking its stiffness. Instead, I get the confirmation that within clearly drawn boundaries, not only I am at my most efficient, but I find an enormous freedom to create. The feeling of security and balance that produces an organised life is perfect terrain for productivity and inspiration. I have been repeatedly criticised by people surrounding me on a personal and professional level that I am too rigid with myself, that I should 'enjoy' life more. 'Live a little!' they say. But these exact rigid life habits let me access a level of ingenuity, an intense life.

I already found the key to creativity, and it does not reside in chaos.

Trying to unlock any door in pitch-black darkness, let alone find the right key on a loaded keyring, is pure suicide.

On motivation and efficiency

_____

The secret for deliberate learning.

PHOTOGRAPHY: JAN DE KONING

Months pass, I make the right choices daily, getting up before sunrise, physically consuming myself for the sake of my vision. When repeating the same method, knowing it's right although results are not as expected, yet when the daily work is becoming difficult to sustain on a psychological level, unshakeable motivation is my salvation. And it's not delivered by post to my door every single morning; I know how precious motivation is and how important it is to cultivate it.

Here are a few notions that help me stay motived.

- *I don't need validation.* I know where I'm going, even if I need to work 18 more months on my own without anyone telling me I'm beautiful, smart, and talented.
- *Every day, I write down the reasons I am pursuing what I'm after.* And by doing so, I remind myself of the importance of even the hardest days of work and training. They count, maybe more than the ones with results and successes. I trained my mind to be able to bear hardship for months.
- *I monitor everything.* The way I feel before and after training, how strong I am on every given day. I have precise values I can compare each day: my fat and body weight, the exactitude of my technique, every single detail of my Art and well-being, the exact amount of macronutrients I've consumed each day in which form and at what time, and their impact on my blood sugar. I have a precise plan for everything that matters: health, training, timings, technique. I know which actions create which outcomes. I am in control of the results. I know some goals within the mission will take years to achieve. Having a clear view of the

big picture and knowing which string to pull if needed is extremely empowering, therefore motivating.

- *I feed my inspiration in line with my mission.* I find that inspiration in music, visual art, books, and philosophy. I feel most alive when immersed in beauty.
- *My self-worth does not depend on results.* I am extremely solid as a person; therefore, I rarely lose my balance. Rigour is reassuring. I question my assumptions daily, but external attributes don't have the power to make me doubt myself and lose motivation.

EXPIRATION DATE

The expiration date of a physical performer is a pressing reality. Every year matters, a lot more than in most other fields. Not only do you have to look fresh and young onstage, but your body, your tendons, and ligaments have a given amount of usage before they let you down.

Your training should take that into consideration. The 10,000 hours rule—saying it needs 10,000 hours of practice to become an expert at anything—is an incomplete idea. Of course, hard work is essential to develop skills, but if not performed appropriately, it is more damaging than helpful. Every time you repeat a traumatic movement, you remove time on your list. Every time you perform that contortion, you use your body in a premature way. Choose wisely the way you train. Every single time I go on my hands, I choose to give the best of myself as I'm using time in that possibility window. I do not use hours of training for the sake of it. Practice doesn't make perfect; perfect practice makes perfect.

Elite performers don't just practise, they practise deliberately. Deliberate practice requires a level of effort and commitment that can only be justified by one outcome: improving your skills. It's not particularly pleasant; it's intensively energy-consuming and might not be amusing for its own sake. The thrill is to know you are getting closer to your perfection. Deliberate practice commands clear goals and a level of consistency that only extreme discipline can bring. The self-investment goes far beyond simple rehearsals.

Remove from your life or delegate anything that does not help your mission.

Give up any casual social life. The time you spend with other human beings matters; pick them wisely. Be the opposite of a people pleaser.

Help yourself making the right choices. I travel with my own food; there is no time to find a place that suits my dietary needs before a show or in an airport.

Cultivate minimalism; let go of useless belongings. They will make you a slave to moving them around the globe or even taking care of them.

Avoid physical—including virtual—business meetings. Prioritise written communication. People are more concise in this way than when you let them talk. And when they speak in front of others during a meeting involving more persons, it usually evolves into a 15-seconds-of-glory power game.

If you want to be a pro at something, act like one. Take yourself seriously. If you don't, no one will.

Chapter 6

Stress management

_____

When what you want is on the other side of fear.

Friend or enemy? Stress is a magnificent animal if you can tame it. If you can't, it has the power to destroy a career, a personality, a life.

Today, stress is one of my most precious tools—it's an invaluable indicator of risk, and when the butterflies-in-the-stomach feeling manifests, I know I'm facing something worth my time and energy. But that hasn't always been the case. I had to learn how to deal with stress when the stakes are high and still perform at my best.

My first encounter with it was at age 13. I was undertaking a prominent performance for a big fundraising gala—my first time being broadcast on TV. The act my partner and I were to perform involved a fair amount of risk. I was terrified when executing some of the moves—twisting in the air, four metres above the ground. It was only the rehearsals, and my hands were already sweating with nerves. Was I ready?

On the day, I delivered a disappointing performance. I slightly changed my technique out of fear of falling, unintentionally creating more risk. The result was mediocre. I didn't know it at the time, but I'd let myself react to the fear when I should have been solid and consistent. If I'd just done what I'd practised hundreds of times, it would have kept the mistakes at bay. I hated that stage experience. In fact, falling asleep the night before, I had secretly wished it would be cancelled. It was absurd since I had been looking forward to it for weeks. It should have been a brilliant opportunity to treasure for life.

I'd been training to execute death-defying stunts but not to bear the pressure that came with it.

I knew I needed to find an answer to the situation; a way to analyse it. And so began my quest into understanding and conquering stress. I pored over every sports psychology book I could find in the public library. Every detail of that first experience had been way too unpleasant, and I had no intention of living that experience a second time.

The fruit of my readings taught me that, 'Stress is your body's natural reaction to any change that requires an adjustment'. If I could learn to control my physical, mental, and emotional responses, I could turn stress into an ally. And what if I could even turn this into a positive experience?

We perceive stress as inherent to a given situation, but it's also a choice, and ultimately a privilege (yet again). Once you know how to host it, and once you understand the power you have over it, the advantage is suddenly in your hands. It's your reaction to it that matters; you can change it to work in your favour.

I soon noticed that stress carries bidirectional components: the reactions it physically provokes on the body—shortness of breath, cold and stiff hands, accelerated heartbeat, upset digestive system, tensed and rigid muscles—with practice and awareness, can be controlled to lower the level of stress. My balance and acrobatic capabilities are so impaired by these physical reactions that I can't let it happen. I need to physically be extremely calm when I step onstage to deliver a performance. By consciously putting myself in the right physical state—breathing normally, relaxing my face muscles, keeping my limbs and hands fluid and in movement—I noticed part of the stress vanishes.

My first experience with fear onstage was dwarfed on numerous occasions later in my career, although I've always been a very composed performer. The more my craft and career upgraded, the higher the level of stress involved. But it became part of my life and my working experience, and I became a master at handling it. The better I became at handling it, the higher I climbed on the scale of success. The circle would never end. Now, when a problematic situation arises, my visceral reaction is: *Let the fun begin*!

TRAIN YOUR MIND TO REACT THE RIGHT WAY TO STRESSFUL SITUATIONS

1. Stress must be rationalised

Start by calculating the risks: Break down every single risk factor related to the situation to the smallest details. What do you fear? What would be the worst-case scenario? By analysing and understanding each stressor in detail, you'll realise that, in most cases, the worst enemy is still a very manageable one.

2. Prepare accordingly

Consider all the possible consequences and find a solution to every potential hiccup. A solid plan is needed for every possibility, no matter how unlikely it may be. Where there's no clear solution, make a decision: either go ahead with the possibility of facing that particular risk or, if the risks are too high for the reward—in my case, this could mean falling to my death—then simply abort the project. No doubt, no regret.

3. Confront the fear

Once you've developed the tools and put plans in place to respond to every possible risk factor, it's time to confront that very event that creates stress. Usually, once you've broken down the potential stressors to small entities, the remaining fears are not relevant anymore. You are in control.

4. Follow the plan of response

Adrenaline is a powerful drug, providing us with a (fake) superhero cape. Stress makes us do things we might not otherwise do. But if you've already decided how you'll react if your fears do come to fruition, you just have to follow the plan of action. This isn't rocket science, but when the stakes are high, our minds tend to tell us our dedicated planning was wrong or that a different course of action is better. I consider both messages as part of an 'adrenaline-induced syndrome'. In either case, listening to these impulsive thoughts in a state of stress is a beginner's mistake. Keep faith in your plan and react according to your previously strategised response. Because once stress hits, you are in no condition to make a better decision.

I regard pressure and stress as privileges: the stress-free moments of my life have never been the most meaningful ones. And if I refer to 'Stress is just your body's natural reaction to any change that requires an adjustment', that adjustment might as well mean improvements. I no doubt prefer the uncomfortable side of the line.

6.1

Flying for a living

Wishful thinking is not a strategy.

PHOTOGRAPHY: ANTONIO NAPOLI

S tress—and my steadfast response to it—has saved my life a few times in my career. When you perform 25 metres above the ground without a security line for a living, you must learn to not only deal with stress but to put yourself in a very specific state when responding to extreme stressors.

In 2013, after two decades performing aerially at eight, 10, or 12 metres off the ground, I was to perform in front of 50,000 people in an enormous football stadium. I would be doing something I'd never done before—literally flying on a bunch of helium balloons, 30 metres above the ground, with only my own strength and a sheer piece of fabric to hold onto. The preparation for the performance threw up considerable stressors. The importance of the event and the amount of uncertainty that surrounded it both raised my stress levels to a new high.

There were a lot of obstacles to consider:

- A last-minute change in the music because of royalty concerns. That might not sound like a big issue, but in a *Physical Poetry* performance, every single movement is timed to the music. It gives a precise structure not only to the performer but also to the ground technical team.

- Instead of a fixed anchoring point, I'd be performing on a moving one—the cluster of helium balloons. I had never practised executing already difficult movements while floating about—left, right, up, and down.

- I was performing 15 metres higher than I had ever experienced. Being outside and at a great height meant there was a risk of wind blowing into the aerial silks I was holding onto, possibly making them escape my grip.

- The biting cold of Germany in November contrasted with my picky requirements for a minimum of 24

Celsius (75 Fahrenheit) while performing. Would my hands be weakened or numbed by cold?

- The show was being broadcast live—an additional mental stress. I now had to act for the camera projecting my image across huge screens as well as physically performing my routine for a distant audience—I'd have to act big and small at the same time.
- My technical team had a reduced amount of preparation time to set up the flying structure due to the football half-time chronometers. If we weren't ready to go in five minutes sharp, in comparison to our usual 40, the show would be cancelled—and my client, as well as the sponsors, had a lot to lose.

After taking all these stressors into account (1. *Stress must be rationalised*), I prepared well to deal with every single one (2. *Prepare accordingly*). I examined every possible problematic situation. I put security plans in place if I didn't feel comfortable for any reason whilst in the air and a way to communicate it visually to my ground team. I specifically practised how long I could experience cold and found a way to keep my hands warm. As the meteorological conditions would make my skin dryer, I tested the difference I would experience in grip while holding onto the aerial fabric. We had a team and trained helpers ready to get us through with reduced preparation time. We had strict visual cues, all overseen by my assistant, to ensure the smoothness and security of the preparation. One trusted technician was appointed to do nothing but supervise the process and to give me security updates every 60 seconds. Everything had been rehearsed in case something unexpected happened.

Ultimately, I was going to do it (3. *Confront the fear*). I would be performing acrobatic stunts at 30 metres high, flying on a moving helium structure without a net.

Ten minutes prior to take off, I was completely warmed up, stretched, muscularly activated, made up, and ready to go. I was covered under a winter jacket and wearing warming gloves and boots. I'd remove the extra layers 30 seconds before my performance to reveal my tiny unitard—any additional clothing can disrupt my movements, so I have to wear a thin costume that shows a lot of skin. I would then wrap myself up in the aerials silks to be securely thrown 25 metres high and perform my first movement.

When we reached the five-minute mark, my team started to work as planned, assembling the balloon cluster to which I'd hook my aerial silks. Everything was going smoothly. A strange silence reigned in our team; everyone fully concentrated on the task. I had requested a time update every 30 seconds. We were running on schedule, two-and-a-half minutes before take-off: time to attach my aerial equipment to the helium balloons. No one but my head technician was allowed near me during this process—no risk of mistakenly sabotaging my knot. I was in constant communication with my team, proceeding calmly. I removed my boots, gloves, and winter jacket, feeling the biting cold hitting my body, and started wrapping myself in the silks.

Suddenly, I hear men screaming. There seems to be a problem on the field. Keeping my breathing rhythm low against a background of intensifying panic and screams, I assess the situation and get dressed back into my warm clothes after informing my helper to keep an eye on the aerial silks, now hooked to the structure. I never remove my eyes from my equipment when the show is imminent. But we only have two minutes left before take-off or we'll lose our advertisement spot on prime-time TV—and our slot to perform. I know we are losing time; *we'll need to use plan B if I want to fly at all, I thought.* Time is running, and a team is still loudly negotiating the issue a few metres away from me.

I remain calm. My heart rate doesn't accelerate, and my head is crisp and clear. I trust my plan; I trust my team; I trust my skills. When I receive the go-ahead to fly, we have 18 seconds left before the live TV broadcasts my image to millions of viewers. Everyone on my team gives their ready sign. Men are still screaming in the background, but I push the sound to the back of my head so my focus can remain on the verbal cues of my assistant. I drop my winter jacket to the ground. I visually inspect my equipment for any security glitch. There is no time to wrap myself into the silks as planned; plan B it will be (4. *Follow the plan of response*). I hold tight onto the silks like my life depends on it—and give the signal: YES. I'm propelled 25 metres in the air.

Becoming elite is not just about skills; it's also about learning to handle these situations and learning to be impermeable to negative messages. I'm not immune to the 'you will fall' or 'you will fail' thoughts; I just don't let them influence me when they show up. Stressful episodes aren't the time to open an emotional door—let that come later if it has to. Do not allow any change of focus.

No one cares about how good you were yesterday during practice. No one cares about all the reasons you couldn't deliver greatness today. Deal with your weaknesses beforehand. You need to give your best the moment the world is looking.

Excellence can only be reached by increasing mental strength.

PART 2

Health

Chapter 7

Genetically malleable

Biofeedback for performance and longevity.

Who wants a killer body with a visible six-pack, slender looking toned legs, ageless skin, insatiable energy, more flexibility, no pain?

Me too!

And in my line of work, all the above aren't vanity; they are requisite.

The good news is, by endlessly repeating simple daily choices, they become reachable. Understanding that fact; I decided to commit an enormous amount of my time and energy into getting to know my body in-depth and doing what was needed to reach my physical goals. Becoming my own guinea pig—sometimes making monumental mistakes—I fast-forwarded my personal discovery to become an elite performer, often against all odds. At times during my career, I chose to lower my body fat to 6.8% to be able to achieve specific movements, for increased functional results. I'll go more in-depth on the subject later. It's more important first to understand the most valuable component of most physical and health-related goals.

NATURE AND NURTURE

We are not condemned to the body we have; we are not entirely sentenced to the health troubles we experience, even through genetics. We are, though, definitely constrained by mental laziness and the lack of willpower to take the actions needed to achieve the body we'd gladly pay for. I've made it a lifelong quest to keep fine-tuning my habits to achieve my best health, inside and out. My daily choices were previously made almost exclusively to push my physical boundaries—lower fat, boost muscle and strength—and remain elite in my field. Nowadays, I extend my quest to general health and longevity.

What if you wanted to enhance your genetic baggage to a better one? Thanks to epigenetics—the study of our actions influencing the manifestation of these genes—this question is not as irrational as it sounds. Our health is influenced by both our DNA and our life regimen. We do have a precise genetic code, but the expression of these genes—the way they work—is partially controlled by lifestyle: what you eat, the environment in which you live, how you sleep, how you exercise. These factors can cause chemical modifications around the genes that will turn them on or off over time. These alterations don't change the DNA sequence per se, but they may alter how cells 'read' genes. It is shifting the way we look at auto-immune diseases, among other facts. We do have the power to play with our genetic baggage.

About 70% of our immune system is in our intestine[1], which reacts directly to the food we eat—a simple reason why there's no one-diet-fits-all. Even the slightest intolerance can sabotage a health regimen if we keep eating the wrong food. Additionally, to maintain a lifestyle that allows you to reach elite physical goals for a lifetime, you have to find a way to make it pleasurable. Not only are we all individuals with a single set of genes, but we all have unique preferences. You won't persevere eating food you hate or practising a sport you can't stand. And without consistency, you won't see results. What's good for me isn't necessarily good for you.

Your appearance on the outside shows years of daily choices led by a strong personality. Short-term pain for long-term benefits is easy to understand, but you first have to bear the short-term pain: build strength and resilience. There is an enormous psycho-

---

1   Nutrient Tasting and Signaling Mechanisms in the Gut. II. The intestine as a sensory organ: neural, endocrine, and immune responses. John B. Furness, Wolfgang A. A. Kunze, and Nadine Clerc. 01 NOV 1999https://doi. org/10.1152/ajpgi.1999.277.5.G922

logical factor to succeeding at looking good, as absurd as that may sound. I suspect most of us know we should eat healthily and be more active, and the basics of what that means is mere common sense. So why aren't we all lean, healthy, and energized?

Lack of information or laziness?

What are the specifics—perfect diet, training, and life habits—to reach peak levels of health, performance, and body composition (looking ripped)?

The bad news is that there is no single guide that works and a lot of sometimes conflicting—and always confusing—information to unscramble.

You have to design the pilot for yourself. And, you will have to update it ever so slightly, continuously, for the rest of your life. Your body is in permanent evolution; what works now won't necessarily work in six months or 10 years. The same goes for fat loss and pain/inflammation management. In fact, athletes keep changing their training as their bodies adapt, and the training designed a few weeks or months ago becomes irrelevant.

I grew up in an athletic culture where listening to your body's needs and signs—for instance, pain—was seen as being weak or overly protective. I've learned to push through severe injuries, sometimes performing on partially torn ligaments and muscles just for the sake of the next show, because it was a way to show courage and determination—*the show must go on* taken to a ridiculous level. Complaining or taking care of one's body was considered being whiny. As a child and teenager, this mindset did irreparable damage to my body. Now, after more than three decades pushing the machine to higher levels, I am the complete opposite, and the results show. I would never have envisioned being in a better physical condition in my thirties than any time before. I would never have even dared to think I could keep improving the *Phys-*

ical Poetry on such an acrobatic and physical level decades later. I diligently learned to understand every single body cue to use it for better performance. That goes for pain response, fatigue, body ache, energy, immune system response, endurance, and stamina. For all the above, I have a precise test and scale to compare on a regular basis. I note everything in detail.

BODY AWARENESS

To lead an inhuman rhythm of life, be healthy, and have a spectacular body, you must learn to listen to yourself and understand your metabolism through (un)obvious and precise signs and reactions. That, in addition to a deeper knowledge of your health, will lead you to real results. When faced with inadequate fitness results or poor health, the reaction is to search for quick fix or answers from whoever is an authority or seems more knowledgeable than ourselves. That is the first mistake. Pretending that a doctor, a fitness guru, or an Olympic athlete who just wrote his or her latest bestseller can give you an accurate answer without having studied *you* in-depth—for years—is choosing to gamble with your health. You are the only inhabitant in your body; paying attention is essential. There are no shortcuts; you must apply a lifetime of attentiveness to correlate it to adequate results. You need to know yourself enough to find your answers in slight modifications in physical responses. That may sound daunting, but that too eventually becomes automatic.

One of the most significant teachers in an athlete's career is his or her own physiological feedback. Developing a precise understanding of your body's way of expression, through pain and experiences, is one of your most valuable assets to improve your performance, general physical condition, and well-being. It will help you catch any possible hitch and fix it at such an early stage that it doesn't become a problem. As a soloist performing for big productions around the globe, I can't afford a cold, a superficial infection, a bad day at work. To perform an eight-minute aerial routine with a blocked nose is not only unpleasant, it is potentially dangerous. My clients expect me to step onstage and be at my best, and so do I.

Body awareness involves sensory awareness—the ability to identify and experience inner physical sensations (e.g. a tight muscle) and the overall physiological state of the muscles (e.g. relaxed, tense). If you have spent a lifetime working with your body as your primary tool, you might know the feeling of breaking down every single aching movement, angle, type, and intensity of pain to understand better the 'state of affairs'. For many years, my very first thought upon awakening in the morning was: 'How painful?'

From my bed, I would proceed to mentally scan my whole body without moving. I would then further examine every discomfort, recurrent pain, and known injury to determine how I could adjust my training to get the most out of it or simply get moving despite the pain. I haven't always been reasonable, fearing that one day of reduced exercise, even if due to an injury, would compromise my future results for a given performance. I couldn't stomach the idea of skipping a day of practice. I heavily abused my body for years until I slowly learned, oftentimes through grim circumstances and outcomes, to develop a two-way relationship with it and get the best out of natural biofeedback.

Anti-inflammation lifestyle

Diet, sleep, training, and manual therapy.

PHOTOGRAPHY: DAVID CANNON

At some point in my career, I had accepted the idea that it's just *that* painful. Waking up in the morning and not being able to touch your toes is a little unexpected for a contortionist. I thought others had just learned to not bother the rest of the world with their physical discomfort, and so did I. I had no major diagnosed injury that made it acceptable for me to lie down a few times a day to lessen the lower back pain. I thought my spine or other joints becoming visibly swollen must be a defence mechanism to make me stop bending incessantly. I thought I could live with it. I did not know it was possible to sleep an entire night on your side or stomach and still be able to move your neck the next day.

For years, I had so much inflammation in my hips, neck, shoulders, and lower back that I couldn't physically stay still for more than 10 minutes without a level of discomfort so high I couldn't hold a simple conversation. My psychological energy was redirected towards pain management, even unconsciously. During intercontinental flights, I had to get up and stretch every half hour. I grew used to avoiding handshakes by any imaginative way. The squeeze it created on the metacarpal bones of my hands was like someone stabbing me each time. These examples are not exceptional; they are only some of the many cases of the price to pay to achieve an elite performance status and the work behind it. The body is not made for this!

I pushed my joints through impossible stress sessions for decades, six to eight hours per day. I inevitably had to make up for their premature ageing and excessive inflammation level. I had surrendered to the mistaken idea that this pain had to be part of my life, until one day a personal issue kept me from training for nine consecutive days and suddenly everything stopped—temporarily—aching so much.

I was craving getting back to my usual training and performance routine, but I had also tasted a relatively pain-free few days and the psychological freedom of not nursing pain all day long. I had to find a new strategy to train as hard or even more and suffer less. I hated the idea that pain was somehow dictating my performance and its limits. Ultimately, it would restrict my career. Although I had raised the threshold of the amount I could bear, it was often discomfort due to inflammation, and not fatigue, that governed when to stop a day of training and that became impossible to accept. Slowing down my pace of life or quantity of training was not an option; I was nowhere near satisfied with the effort and number of hours I committed to my craft. I needed to practice harder and better to reach the level I was striving for. My dedication needed to be taken a step further though.

I committed to finding every tiny detail I could add, subtract, or modify to my daily routine to decrease inflammation and speed up regeneration. From the exact formula of macronutrients to eat to make me secrete more growth hormone—promoting repair of daily tissue damage—to intensity of cardio to maximize blood flow without tapping into overuse: I would dig deeper into everything health-related I had left unaddressed. I started diligently taking care of the most important spheres to address to decrease inflammation while raising the fitness level: diet—including hydration and supplementation—sleep, training, and manual therapy.

Stressing my body so much daily, the response following a sugary meal or a lousy night's sleep is sometimes so violent that pain level is a good reminder of the importance of making the right choices. It serves as a well-deserved slap in the face when discipline alone hasn't done its job. I already had a relatively good diet, but I stopped eating everything that triggered inflammation in my body, even the slightest intolerance.

To find your optimum diet, you first have to investigate. Test every suspect food by removing it from your diet for two weeks at a time—without changing anything else—and remain attentive to changes, if any. Removing is not reducing; stopping is forgetting it even exists.

Drastic? Perhaps, Efficient? Absolutely!

I do not believe in so-called 'cheat days'. Why would you need to *cheat* on food that makes you feel amazing and fulfilled? Why *cheat* yourself? Having a healthy lifestyle is not a sacrifice: If you lack the willpower to stick to it, train your willpower.

As a side note, so-called cheat days sometimes account for a number of calories so high it sabotages a six-days-out-of-seven excellent diet and cancels all fat loss results. If you are unable to sustain your daily diet and need to binge once in a while, there is a problem in your daily diet in the first place. Don't build it on a bad foundation.

Once you establish a plan, stick to it. Your goal is to make it as straightforward as possible until you do not have to think about which healthy choices to make. I even tricked myself into learning to love food that would do me well, moving from a sugar-addicted, frozen-meal aficionado teenager to a clean eater today. Complicated actions today will become habits tomorrow.

Consider your health as a company; you need a strong business plan.

- How do you want to feel and look in two months, one year, 10 years?
- Which specific actions do you have to take daily to get there and stay there?
- Would you willingly delay results for the sake of an action (i.e. eating unhealthy food, skipping your morning run) that gives you immediate gratification?

After you establish where you want to be and have a clear list of priorities to undertake, apply the first step consistently until it is integrated; then move to the second step. Each desired health change eventually becomes part of your life hygiene.

THE ANTI-INFLAMMATION BASICS: DIET

The role that nutrition plays in the inflammation process is greatly underestimated. A careless diet translates into pain, joint restriction, and a possible performance debilitation, let alone weight increase. For anyone who doesn't train excessively, the effect of a bad diet might translate into a headache, mild joint pain, or eventually arthritis and the manifestation of an auto-immune disease. In the end, inflammation is an enemy for everyone.

I have a nutritious breakfast with proteins and healthy fats. I suggest skipping the starches and dairy products; they naturally promote inflammation for many. A high ratio of carbs makes my blood glucose oscillate too much. I'm physically more performant when I keep it below 50% of my morning calorie consumption.

Despite the overwhelming amount of information available on diet and lifestyle, small changes can make a big difference in the inflammatory process. A natural law that prevails is only eat real food. It's essential to learn to read food labels and not ingest products if they contain terms you don't recognise. Avoid anything processed, fried, packaged, refined, or high in unknown substances.

It is now proven and reported that processed sugars and other high-glycaemic starches increase inflammation markers in the blood. In contrast, an increased amount of good fat produces an anti-inflammatory effect on our bodies. All fats aren't the same: omega-6's are pro-inflammatory, while omega-3's have an anti-inflammatory effect. Load your diet with raw nuts and seeds, avocados, olive oil, cold-water wild fish such as salmon, tuna, herring, mackerel, and sardines. Eat plenty of colourful fruits and vegetables containing high amounts of ascorbic acid (vitamin C) as well as food filled with vitamin E, including nuts, seeds, and green leafy vegetables.

Here is a list of basic pro-inflammatory nutrients to avoid:

- Most white starches
- Refined sugar: sucrose, glucose, fructose, maltose, dextrose, evaporated cane juice, high fructose corn syrup—molasses, honey, fruit juice concentrates, and lactose may also produce an inflammatory response.
- Alcohol, especially beer and sweet cocktails
- Vegetable oils rich in omega-6: soybean oil, corn oil, sunflower oil
- Artificial sweeteners such as aspartame

If you want precise results from your diet, measure or weigh everything you consume, not only to restrict portions but to make sure you eat the right amount of the right food and avoid the guessing game on grams of proteins, lipids, and carbohydrates consumed. Overeating isn't good for anyone, but the lack of proper nutrients is the enemy of regeneration.

SUPPLEMENTATION

When it comes to supplementation, as with diet, no formula fits all—one must personalise. High-quality multi-vitamins, omega-3, vitamin D, and magnesium are on the top of my list. Additionally, I take a good source of collagen protein to provide the right amino acids. To design an effective supplementation program, one has to take into account gender, age, level of activity, environmental triggers, and genetics. A precise blood panel is necessary to go into more detail.

HYDRATION

Dehydration is one of the most basic and overlooked causes of disease. Even a body in a mild state of dehydration can produce an acute inflammatory response. Simply drinking water and staying hydrated at all times will improve your quality of life and decrease all types of pain. Ingesting magnesium in food or as a supplement will also help your body to stay properly hydrated. I keep a huge bottle of water with me throughout the day. Some consider that I water-binge! If you need an extra incentive to drink more, you can add some fresh mint leaves or fruit.

SELF-HEALING

Always take the extra 20 minutes to stretch after a practice or performance. This is non-negotiable even when there is a greeting or photoshoot post-performance waiting. This step—known as cool down—and its benefit is underestimated. It saves not only discomfort the next morning but potentially a few years of career. You can release most muscular tension by doing soft isometric stretches, performed *on a warm body*. Stretching, if done correctly, is one of the most powerful self-healing techniques. When stretching a given area, make sure to move in and out of the stretch very gently and maintain it for at least thirty seconds. Listen to your body, reach an uncomfortable level, but never a state of pain.

*Side note: Extreme flexibility technique is a whole different animal. In order to reach extreme—not functional—levels of flexibility, you have to follow an intense and specific training. In no means would I consider this a cooldown or rehabilitation practice. It is made to enhance flexibility to extreme levels for sports or arts such as rhythmic gymnastics, classical dance, and contortion. It is not meant to reach a functional level and can easily become destructive to the joints, especially when not properly paired with strengthening in the hyperextension.

SLEEP

A lack of sleep will put anyone in an inflammatory state. If you're triggered by inflammation due to an active lifestyle or stress exposure, you need quality sleep as a priority treatment. The more you exercise, the more you should sleep. I personally need seven hours if not very physically active and from nine to 10 when on a full training regimen. Even healthy volunteers show elevated inflammatory markers and experience increased pain when exposed to sleep restriction. If you want to raise your athletic level or fitness look (gain muscle/lose fat), sleep must be part of the equation.

Most people rarely sleep enough or drink enough water.

CARDIO EXERCISING

It might sound counterintuitive to exercise when you suffer from joint stiffness, pain, or any kind of muscular soreness. Still, a light aerobic exercise, such as a fast incline walk, will help oxygenate your body and activate blood flow. As a result, it will reduce inflammation, speed up recovery and decrease pain. Avoid any activity that creates a repetitive impact on joints—boxing, running, plyometrics—preferring fast incline walking, biking, or elliptical. Although it will promote it, the primary purpose I address in this case is not fat loss.

WILLPOWER FAILURE

The difference between success and failure does not only reside in your willpower but also in your preparation. There will be days where triggers are high, where you will be tired and susceptible to making the wrong choices. Anticipate these weaker moments and do not allow doubt to come into your new space. Do not keep food you don't want to eat at home and never compromise on your schedule. Plan every meal and training session beforehand, removing any extra steps. What if you had to go out and pick up a toothbrush at the store every morning; is there a chance you would postpone teeth brushing for a few hours or even skip it sometimes?

Write down your health goals for the day and the week, every day, forever!

Extra health tools

Hot or cold, eating or not?

I have been a sauna user for years. Not only for the exposure to hot temperatures that relax muscle contractions—and feels good—but also to help post-training recovery, increase endurance, muscle mass, and strength.

THERMAL STIMULI

Choose dry sauna as compared to a steam bath for its added cardiovascular benefits[2]. Aim for at least three rounds of 10 minutes punctuated with five to 10 minutes of cooling. Time it immediately after training for its profound effect on boosting growth hormone[3]. The body produces growth hormone more prominently after exercising and during sleep. As the name suggests, it stimulates growth, cell reproduction, and cell regeneration. It is highly coveted by athletes and the anti-ageing business.

Sauna also reduces chronic inflammation—that's the invisible inflammation. Chronic inflammation occurs on a cellular level. It is known to have an important role in the development of many chronic diseases. Sauna use has been shown to significantly reduce the blood levels of C-reactive protein, one of the blood proteins that rise during an acute inflammatory phase. On the other hand, sauna use increases heat shock proteins that play an essential role in many cellular processes needed for recovery[4].

2   Hussain, Joy, and Marc Cohen. 2018. "Clinical Effects of Regular Dry Sauna Bathing: A Systematic Review Evidence-Based Complementary and Alternative Medicine". DOI: 10.1155/2018/1857413. (https://www.hindawi.com/journals/ecam/2018/1857413/)

3   Ftaiti, Foued, Monem Jemni, Asma Kacem, Monia Ajina Zaouali, Zouhair Tabka, Abdelkarim Zbidi, and Laurent Grélot. 2008. "Effect of hyperthermia and physical activity on circulating growth hormone". *Applied Physiology, Nutrition, and Metabolism* DOI:10.1139/h08-073. https://dx.doi.org/10.1139/H08-073

4   Yamada, Paulette M., Fabiano T. Amorim, Pope Moseley, Robert Robergs, and Suzanne M. Schneider. 2007. "Effect of heat acclimation on heat shock protein 72 and interleukin-10 in humans". *Journal of Applied Physiology*. DOI: 10.1152/japplphysiol.00242.2007.

The extreme thermal stressors—high or low temperature—are a valuable tool for healing if used appropriately. As long as I can remember, I've been using ice application on injured parts of my body or after joint overuse due to an intense training session or performance, extending the benefit to prevention. Ice pack use is an everyday occurrence for athletes.

I started reading more in-depth medical literature in the field of anti-inflammatory lifestyle and possible ways to reverse injuries judged 'irreversible' as well as chronic joint inflammation. Apart from the more invasive stem-cell therapy and platelet-rich plasma (PRP) in regenerative medicines, my research kept leading me back to cryotherapy—the practice of exposing the body or specific areas of the body—to extremely cold temperatures for defined periods. I was in pain due to a very hectic performing and travelling schedule, allowing me less time for a balanced lifestyle and adequate preventive training. I decided to get over my repulsion of cold and see for myself if its miracles were real.

Every single evening, I take a long, hot bath before going to bed. One evening I switched to a mild to eventually a cold shower. At first, it was excruciating discomfort, but then for the first time in weeks, my lower back pain did not prevent me from falling asleep.

Coincidence, perhaps?

Like everything else, it requires practice. I eventually kept training my cold resistance until I could comfortably stand for three minutes in an icy shower or bath. Having five kilograms (11 pounds) of ice cubes delivered to my hotel room to plunge into an ice bath post-performance became a habit.

The most significant benefit I noted was decreased inflammation in my lower back, hips, and shoulder area. I could also return to full muscular training sooner, with reduced soreness and pain.

Cold therapy on athletes is known for its direct and powerful effect on recovery[5]. As unpleasant as it can be, a full-body cold bath will reduce inflammation by constricting blood vessels, draining the blood, ridding the body of toxins and lactic acid build-up. As you climb out of a cold bath, your system provides a fresh flow of nutrient-rich blood to aid recovery. Another benefit of cold exposure is the psychological feeling of well-being. It is thought to be induced by an increased production of norepinephrine, a hormone and neurotransmitter partially responsible for a good mood. There is a precise timing to follow to optimise cold therapy effects. The exposure also depends on body composition, type of sports practised, and the desired outcomes.

My best results are achieved when exposing myself for sessions of three minutes, with 15-minute pauses in between to warm up my body, although a single exposure produces enough benefits for me to notice. Research also shows that cold exposure may affect lipid metabolism and increase fat loss since energy—calories—is used to reheat the body.

FASTING

In my quest to further help lower my inflammation levels, I have flirted with different fasting methods. Initially, I was not an avid user, but science taught me to pay attention to its perks. Time-restricted eating, in several ways similar to intermittent fasting (IF), is the practice of limiting the hours of food consumption in a given window of the day without reducing calorie intake. Having initially gained a lot of popularity in Silicon Valley by self-proclaimed biohackers, medical research is moving fast in this field. I'm happy

---

5   Lombardi, Giovanni, Ewa Ziemann, and Giuseppe Banfi. 2017. "Whole-Body Cryotherapy in Athletes: From Therapy to Stimulation. An Updated Review of the Literature". *Frontiers in Physiology*. DOI: 10.3389/fphys.2017.00258.

to benefit from the scientific knowledge now available to everyone, but the results remain the same since I've started the practice years ago. I do not personally believe in prolonged fasting unless you suffer from a medical condition for which it has proven helpful. On a psychological level, it doesn't make sense to me to deprive one's body of nutrients and energy for a prolonged period—more than 24 hours—without a proper reason to do so.

I see time-restricted eating as a lifestyle to adopt. You may stick to an eight, 10, or 12-hour feeding window—the time between the first and the last calorie intake of the day. Reducing the hours of feeding and augmenting the hours of fasting on each 24-hour period will be beneficial to your health. Many repair hormones work better when not in digestive mode. The metabolism loves the downtime of not using energy for digestion. A simple apple before bedtime will decrease growth hormone production during the night. More elite athletes are now sticking to this technique. It may sound counter-intuitive as we have been told for decades that muscle growth comes with feeding every three hours—body-builder's style—in order to keep your metabolism running, build muscles, and keep burning calories. Several studies show a completely different picture: it is now scientifically documented that these short-term fasts will boost your metabolism and maintain muscle mass and its functions.

The metabolic benefit in restricting feeding hours is real. Health effects may include decreased fat tissues, increased lean muscle mass, reduced inflammation, better cellular metabolism, augmented repair processes, and improved aerobic stamina[6]. Per-

---

6   Flipping the Metabolic Switch: Understanding and Applying Health Benefits of Fasting (https://www.ncbi.nlm.nih.gov/pmc/articles/PMC5783752/). Stephen D. Anton,1 Keelin Moehl,2 William T. Donahoo,3 Krisztina Marosi,2 Stephanie Lee,1 Arch G. Mainous, III,4 Christiaan Leeuwenburgh,1 and Mark P. Mattson2,5

sonally speaking, I can correlate a decrease in my inflammation blood markers with a time-restricted eating lifestyle. I do not feel it in my pain level or joint capabilities, but I noticed I can slim down on the same diet consumed in an eight-hour window compared to a 12- to 16-hour window, eating precisely the same food and the same quantity. It always takes me a few days to acclimate to changed mealtimes, but after five to seven days, it becomes natural.

If you are into the practice merely for its weight loss effect, I'd suggest you stop eating early at night. Emotional beings tend to binge in the evenings, not upon waking up. If that's the case, you'll be better served by disregarding the number of fasting hours and simply stop eating after an early dinner. To lose weight, stop snacking at night and save yourself the headache of distilling nitty-gritty habits that are above what you should consider.

You'll benefit more from keeping your last bite as far away from your sleep time as possible. Experts suggest that the earlier the feeding window is in the day, the better the results. I personally like fasted cardio upon wakeup. My energy level is more consistent when my glucose level is not bouncing up and down from digesting the morning meal. My morning training is always more productive and steadier when fasted. Though, I would not particularly advise that but rather, move your eating window to earlier in the day. All in all, time-restricted eating did earn its place in my health toolbox. It is a minor discomfort to adopt.

7.3

Take a breath

How to slow down ageing,
improve your brain structure
and immune system.

PHOTOGRAPHY: DAVID CANNON

From cupping, electric muscle stimulation, imagery, compression therapy, acupressure mats—I have tried, used sporadically, adopted, and given up numerous self-healing techniques throughout the years. When I lived in China and was going through exhausting days of training, stimulation like caffeine or food was nowhere to be found for long hours. I was practising in a room with hundreds of Chinese acrobats from eight to five; there was no place I could hide to lie down and rest during short breaks.

At night in my overheated residence, I dedicated the rest of my waking hours to self-improvements or finding solutions to make these days bearable. I discovered the science of deep breathing and started practising it without expectations. My morning training consisted of four hours of hand-balancing. I would repeat the same exercises hundreds of times in front of my hand-balancing teacher who would once in a while have a micro-reaction and nod her head. At random times, she'd say a word in mandarin which meant 'take a pause'—that gave me a few minutes before she'd be back with her stick counting repetitions for me. I started to use every single break to re-oxygenate my brain and body through breathing exercises. Although I was sceptical at first, I soon noticed it was magical. I now think of it as a vitamin B injection on steroids.

My breathing routine was and still is very simple: I'd walk towards the edge of the room, in front of this tiny window with metal bars and look outside where I could gather as much natural light as possible.

1. Empty the lungs of air
2. Breathe in quietly through the nose for eight seconds
3. Hold the breath for a count of eight seconds
4. Exhale forcefully through the mouth for eight seconds
5. Hold for eight seconds, without breathing in

6. Repeat steps two, three, four and five 10 times, counting very slowly

The practicality of this short fix is that it appears as if I was
looking out the window, incognito. It takes only five minutes and
may have opened my mind to the next step.

MEDITATION

I have tried and quit meditation many times, always with that
bitter aftertaste of failure. I would drink a litre of the most
horrendous liquid every morning if I knew it would improve my
performance as an athlete. Still, unlike other self-torture practice
that I happily carry on with, meditation has been particularly hard
to integrate into my life.

I expected it would bring me peace, focus, and well-being.
Instead, I experienced only discomfort, boredom, and feeling I
was wasting my time. While I was going through my grocery list
during a meditation attempt, I experienced anxiety and frustra-
tion. After repetitive failures, the mere thought of it made me
want to throw plates at the wall.

What I experienced is normal. The harder it is, the more you
probably need it. Although meditation is a learning process for
everyone, many over-doer, high achiever, so-called 'type-A person-
alities' are in the same situation and find it particularly challenging
to overcome. Not so surprising since my *normal* is to train, study
neuroscience via audio, learn a new language, and hold mental
counts in my head, simultaneously. Turning off a few channels
would inevitably be a challenge.

Being an avid reader and learner on brain, neuroscience, and
psychology for my whole adult life, it would have been perplexing

for me not to persist with meditation given the evidence. The scientifically validated reasons to meditate are just too many to ignore.

It enhances your immune function by boosting antibodies. A UCLA study concluded that HIV positive patients who practice mindful meditation slow down the decline of their CD4 cell count[7]. These are the immune cells associated with keeping the virus from propagating; avoiding their natural reduction is lifesaving. Additionally, several findings show that chronic disorders like type-2 diabetes, obesity, heart disease, and high blood pressure are reduced through meditation. A stronger immune system? I'll take that.

It is a proven cure for depression. We often hear about the well-being effects of meditation on mood and depressive states, but has it been officially and medically validated? Researchers at Britain's Oxford University and Plymouth University Peninsula Schools of Medicine and Dentistry conducted the first large-scale study to compare the treatment of chronic depression with Mindfulness-Based Cognitive Therapy (MBCT)[8]—a smart way to say meditation—and anti-depressants. The results show little difference in the outcomes in the meditative solution, minus the unpleasant side effects.

It structurally improves your brain. This, to me, is the most fascinating function of meditation and the one that makes me con-

7   Brain Behav Immun. Author manuscript; available in PMC 2009 Aug 11.
     Published in final edited form as: Brain Behav Immun. 2009 Feb; 23(2):
     184–188. Published online 2008 Jul 19. doi: 10.1016/j.bbi.2008.07.004
     PMCID: PMC2725018 NIHMSID: NIHMS118434 PMID: 18678242
     Mindfulness meditation training effects on CD4+ T lymphocytes in HIV-1
     infected adults: A small randomized controlled trial. J. David Creswell,* Hector F.
     Myers, Steven W. Cole, and Michael R. Irwin

8   Published online 2008 Jul 19. doi: 10.1016/j.bbi.2008.07.004
     PMCID: PMC2725018 NIHMSID: NIHMS118434 PMID: 18678242
     Mindfulness meditation training effects on CD4+ T lymphocytes in HIV-1
     infected adults: A small randomized controlled trial. J. David Creswell,* Hector
     F. Myers, Steven W. Cole, and Michael R. Irwin

sistently stick to it. One mechanism by which meditation protects the brain is through the production of gamma waves—a sign of neuroplasticity linked to a capacity to learn new things and change synapses as a consequence of new behaviours. In other words, it is the ability of your brain to change, grow, and adapt.

Not only is the brain able to modify, but the whole adult nervous system has the capacity for plasticity, and the structure of the brain can change in response to meditative training. A team of scientists at Harvard found that only eight weeks of Mindfulness-Based Stress Reduction (MBSR) increases thickness in the hippocampus—the learning and memory centre of your brain—as well as in other areas that play roles in emotion regulation. It can also reduce brain cell volume in areas responsible for fear, anxiety, and stress: the amygdala.

Neuroimaging studies have begun to explore the neural mechanisms underlying mindfulness meditation practice. The results suggest several changes in grey matter concentration in brain regions involved in learning and memory processes, emotion regulation, and self-referential processing. Meditation has demonstrated improvement in the self-control areas of your brain. These findings probably are behind the fact that most neuroscientists—not illuminated wannabe gurus—now prioritise meditation in their health hygiene.

Mindfulness meditation slows down cellular ageing. The work of Dr Elizabeth Blackburn—a cell biologist who shared the Nobel Prize in Physiology of Medicine in 2009 for her co-discovery of an enzyme called the telomerase—has made impressive discoveries on the matter. Meditation practice may promote mitotic cell longevity, both through decreasing stress hormones and oxidative stress and increasing hormones that may protect the telomeres[9]. The telomere is much like the plastic tips on the ends of shoelaces preventing your chromosomes from deteriorating. If the telomeres are shortened, cells age faster. Although the field of stress-induced cell ageing is young, experts believe meditation may protect your DNA from oxidative damage due to ageing.

Many of us are not familiar with the concrete basics of meditation. We also, as a society, carry some misconceptions—if not full-blown prejudices—on the practice. Meditation isn't just for monks seeking enlightenment. Physiological changes such as the ones mentioned are precisely what my *sceptical self* needed to stop wanting meditation to be useless, so I could get away without it. During practice, feeling all sorts of thoughts and anxiety is normal, especially at the beginning. Once again, you have to go through an improvement process. It will become easier with time.

Masters at meditation and mindfulness don't feel anxiety, fear, and stress the way the rest of us do in our daily lives. They can detach from these feelings, acknowledge their presence, and wave them goodbye. It's probably the way I benefit the most from meditation in my performing career. A minute before stepping onstage for the show of the decade or even while performing 20 metres above the ground, I'm not immune to unwanted messages, irrational fears, or ridiculous but terrorising thoughts. I have experienced live TV shows where I would, during my whole routine, have one very clear image of myself making a false movement and falling on my behind in front of millions of viewers—not the best

9   doi: 10.1111/j.1749-6632.2009.04414.x
      PMCID: PMC3057175   NIHMSID: NIHMS221333   PMID: 19735238
      Can meditation slow rate of cellular aging? Cognitive stress, mindfulness, and telomeres. Elissa Epel, PhD.,1,* Jennifer Daubenmier, Ph.D.,1 Judith T. Moskowitz, Ph.D.,2 Susan Folkman, PhD.,2 and Elizabeth Blackburn, PhD.3

mental state to be in for optimal performance. Meditation slowly makes these messages meaningless; they run in the background, but my mind doesn't pay attention to them. Having a consistent daily practice makes a huge difference in keeping my focus when overly stimulated.

There are many kinds of meditation practices to be explored to find the one that suits you best: mindfulness, transcendental, compassion, mantra, Vipassana, Art of Living, breathing practices, yoga nidra, yoga, insight, loving-kindness, tai chi, etc.

Simply sitting in silence and being aware of your breathing, without forcing it, is meditating. I am more comfortable with that kind of practice. Twice a day for 10 minutes unclutters the brain. I often consider I don't have time to meditate, but if anything, feeling that I don't have time is a clear indicator I should use the extra sharpness that it will get me in order to gain efficiency.

Chapter 8

Monitoring to improve

Random comparisons produce random outcomes.

To fine-tune your health and performance plan, you must recognise precisely what changes create what results. To do so, I monitor a lot of data in my life—a sort of systematic review.

WEIGHT

A measurement that helps understand the general picture. Disregard body mass index (BMI) entirely and keep in mind that weight is a mix of your bone structure, muscles, organs, hydration level, and fat tissues. If you are extremely lean, there might be a more significative variation only due to hydration level in a 24-hour window. Weight variations are indicators to guide you through specific testing, if needed. By the nature of my work and the way I have to lift and carry my weight in precarious positions, I feel the slightest weight change. Even 500 grams (1.1 pound) makes a difference in the more extreme movements. Some of them I'm unable to perform if I carry an extra kilogram (2.2 pounds).

BODY FAT

In order to know your body fat percentage and compare it regularly, rely on good old skinfold callipers—a pair of callipers used to measure the thickness of skinfolds in precise spots of your body to estimate the amount of body fat. With a basic knowledge of anatomy, you can obtain fairly accurate results.

There are a few advanced machines that can be quite precise as well, however, you can rarely use them with consistency. It might sound extraordinary to use one of these devices, but I doubt one will use hydrostatic weighing or a dual-energy X-ray absorptiometry every morning. On the other hand, most simple body fat monitors have a higher error rate or are not capable of differentiating fat from hydration, making the results irrelevant.

PAIN LEVEL: TENDON, LIGAMENTS, AND MUSCLE PAIN

Muscle soreness and joint pain are to be read differently. Learn to distinguish them. The first is often an indicator that you have worked until muscle failure the previous day and will gain strength post-recovery—with the right rest and nutrition. The latter is a sign that something is not right and often leads towards degeneration. The course of treatment is entirely different.

PERFORMANCE: MUSCLE POWER, ENDURANCE, SKILL-SHARPNESS

Go through the same endurance and skills tests every month, following a 48-hour recovery time.

For example, how many chin-ups, suspended pike-ups, push-ups, straddle press up can you perform before failure. How long can you stay on two hands and then on each hand separately? Create a recurrent test adapted to your discipline, sport, or goal, and correlate the results with your training of the previous weeks. Always consider intensity, repetition, and skills. Random comparisons produce random outcomes. Be specific.

DIET

Take note of everything you eat and at what time of the day, being precise and diligent with quantity and quality. Calorie counting is not a myth. You'll gain weight if you eat more calories than you spend; you'll lose weight if you burn more calories than you consume. It's simple math. I modify macronutrients ratio according to my needs of the moment, whether I am travelling and lacking rest or at my studio training for a few weeks.

SLEEP

Monitor the amount, schedule, and quality of your sleep. Sleep is a significant player in recovery and the production of hormones that help tissue repair. Not only should you consider the number of sleeping hours per night, but the schedule on which you sleep, linking it to natural light exposition—another underestimated tool for recovery. It's essential to find your sweet spot to benefit as much as possible from sleep.

Slow-wave sleep (SWS)—often referred to as deep sleep—occurs during stages three and four of non-rapid eye movement sleep (REM) and is thought to be the most restorative of all sleep stages. Most slow-wave activity occurs in the first two sleep cycles (approximately the first three hours of sleep). Establish an optimum sleeping environment and make sure no disruption happens in this early phase. Coffee and alcohol will disturb these important cycles; even if one falls asleep without effort, the quality of your restorative sleep will suffer.

Poor sleep makes you vulnerable to illness, impairs glucose metabolism, and even decreases testosterone levels. It often contributes to a higher calorie consumption as the self-control systems of your brain are compromised when sleep deprived.

A proper pre-bed routine and a good mattress, the right room temperature, and a pitch-black environment will promote quality sleep. Even dim light can suppress melatonin secretion and interfere with your circadian rhythm. You can monitor your sleep with a sleep tracker to understand its patterns—one that hides under the mattress or a wearable one— but more importantly; make sleep a priority.

RECOVERY

Monitor your perceived recovery time following a precise training routine—ideally high-intensity. Then, define a perceived recovery status based on joint aches, muscle soreness, and aerobic performance—I establish mine via a specific endurance and power test movements. Through this system, you can trace soreness and recovery in performance 24, 48, and 72 hours later. That alone indicates the ideal time of recovery to take before an important performance to be in optimal shape. Keep a high-intensity training schedule for the weeks before and decrease a few days ahead of the day you have to be at best.

BIOMARKERS THROUGH BLOOD PANELS

Regularly test a few biomarkers in your blood. Blood draws are great to indicate health problems; using them to enhance performance is slightly more complicated and requires more medical expertise. You can use these indicators to direct your diet and training choices and detect a health problem at an early stage. Use them to improve physical performance and speed up recovery through tiny life habit adjustments. For the zealous, quarterly testing is ideal, but a yearly check is still valuable. It's an accountable tool to detect the slightest sign of overtraining and lead the body towards a perfect state for recovery. Focus on inflammation markers, 'muscle status' markers, metabolism, and hormones.

Here are my personal favourites to test:
- C-Reactive protein
- Leukocytes (white blood cells)
- Homocysteine (Hcy)
- Creatine kinase
- Vitamin D
- Vitamin B12

- RBC magnesium (in red blood cells)
- Cortisol
- Iron
- Vitamin D
- Thyroid hormones
- Growth hormone
- Oestrogen
- Testosterone
- Omega-3

The more information you have and the more precise you are, the easier it becomes to detect a causal effect—not correlation—and modify daily routines to optimise results.

Chapter 9

Overtraining and injuries

_____

'No pain, no gain' is for Rambo-wannabee egos.

Photography: Parish Kohanim

H ave you ever been injured?

That question!

Pull on the same joints repetitively for decades and repeat the same traumatic movements hundreds of times daily, and then ask that question again. Why don't we ask Olympians if they have ever suffered injuries?

Of course, they have!

The question should be: How do you cope with injuries and keep them minor?

Ballet dancers frequently tear their Achilles tendons, skiers their ACL, aerial performers their shoulder rotator cuff tendons. The idea is to avoid it at all costs or be able to juggle mild injuries and inflammation during a career without too much irreversible damage. Once you injure yourself seriously, you might need surgery and the rehabilitation that follows. You will have inner scar tissue adherences that might negatively impact your performance. When your injury fully recovers, if that is a possibility, you will have to start a whole training program only to re-acquire skills you previously considered basic. Recovery time to be able to sit at your desk and recovery time to be able to perform strenuous physical efforts imply completely different timelines.

FIX IT BEFORE YOU BREAK IT: PERFORMING INJURED

A big part of your training should be directed at injury prevention and strengthening, making your body as injury bulletproof as possible while pushing its boundaries. It is a science in itself and deserves the utmost attention.

It is tempting and relatively easy to keep going when the body aches. Not listening to it does not make you strong; it makes you stupid. You must learn to dissociate pain from discomfort. In strength work as in intense stretching sessions, aim for discomfort to the limits of the bearable—your body needs to be pushed to an appropriate level for gains to occur.

To become an elite performer, you may have to learn to bear thresholds of physical distress rational human beings would associate with a near-death experience. There is a paradox in this: We have to learn to push through pain to maintain and acquire strength and skills—which implies training and performing without ever being 100% pain-free—but we must never cross the line that leads to these irreversible injuries. I'm still learning to dance on the edge of the cliff safely.

For example, you can easily keep training and performing with tendinitis and bursitis for years; it's bearable and does not entirely debilitate your performance. However, not to treat tendon inflammation is not only painful, but over time, inflamed tendons become thickened, lumpy, and irregular. Without appropriate rest and time for the tissue to heal, tendons can become permanently weakened and eventually rupture.

I can't stress enough the importance of preventive reinforcement and stabilisation. It is even more important if you are a beginner since your body isn't ready for what you want it to learn. As you age, you need to increase the ratio of time given to preventive training versus stress training. It is utterly boring but the only way to achieve the highest level.

Some skills are worth practising only when all the influencing factors are perfect; otherwise, it's counterproductive. For the movements that potentially harm your body the most, break down the actions and practice all of these to perfection, reducing the amount of repetition of the damaging movement. Once every perfected step is put together, the final result has dramatically improved. It's a smarter way to develop a given skill.

Injuries remain the most critical obstacle of your career. Don't try to fast forward recovery or ignore signs of distress when your body screams or even whispers. By thinking you can push a bit more and buy yourself time, you buy yourself an early expiration date.

OVERTRAINING

Overtraining may manifest in different ways. The most obvious is a sudden drop in performance, becoming fatigued a lot easier, or an increased sensation of effort when performing what usually only means mild training. An elevated resting heart rate is also a good indicator, thus the value of measuring your heart rate every morning when awaking. Do so in a seated position, before coffee, food, or any activity.

Ignoring overtraining symptoms may worsen into restless sleeping, chronic injuries, and extend to depression due to its impact on your hormonal system. It can also manifest itself in a metabolic imbalance. Personally speaking, the latter is a good indicator. My body will start retaining water for no reason; my weight will increase even if I train more and eat less. It's often a sign that the adrenal glands are not able to function correctly due to the extenuating stress they are sustaining. That symptom often accompanies a broad feeling of overall pain in my whole body. Acute inflammation, due to elevated cortisol, can be detected in a blood draw.

Elevated cortisol leads to loss of strength and muscle mass, poor sleep, high levels of anxiety, inability to recover from daily work, and weight increase. If you can't identify the problem, it might be the start of an infernal cycle.

I am all for pushing until we collapse: the fighter mentality of overcoming fear and discomfort daily until we rise to the top. I am allergic to wimps. But there is a part of the mental strength that translates into stopping when it's time to stop. In that case, being the coward is staying on the wrong path and enduring despite the distress signals that sends your body. Get to know the early signs of overtraining and react before you lose months or years of training abilities.

A strategy to avoid overtraining also sits in increasing your body's resilience to efforts. Knowing your limits and stretching them just enough to improve, but not blindly, thus avoiding sabotaging your improvements.

You will over-train earlier by disregarding proper rest post-physical stress. Stressing your body to high levels through exercise requires an increased quality and quantity of care, including plenty of good sleep. Recovery is part of the practice.

Amongst others, here are a few signs you may be overtraining. Beware that you have to compare these signs to your standard indicators to identify a real abnormality. By monitoring correctly, you'll catch the anomaly sooner.

- Elevated resting heart rate
- Extreme fatigue
- Chronic pain and inflammation
- Loss of appetite
- Gaining weight for no specific reason
- Insomnia and restless sleep
- Increased perceived effort
- Loss of strength and muscle mass
- Mood swings, lack of motivation

What to do when it happens:
- Rest completely
- Hydrate profusely
- Be meticulous with your eating

- Avoid sugar, alcohol, coffee, and everything that drains your adrenal glands
- Resume training with mild physical activity only

At the end of the day, maybe the Rambo-wannabees and wimps have more in common than what we previously thought.

Chapter 10

Against the clock

Performing on a world-class level well into your fifties.

PHOTOGRAPHY: ARMOUR PHOTOGRAPHY

I've had the opportunity to train and perform for years alongside the most impressive athletes and artists. While I admired the skills or precise habits in some, I was rarely impressed by a whole living philosophy directed towards performance quality and longevity until I met Dmitrii Arnaoutov.

A CASE STUDY: DMITRII ARNAOUTOV

Dmitrii Arnaoutov has been a world-renowned circus artist for over five decades. He was known to be one of the best Russian cradle flyers in the Soviet Union for many years. He won the Crystal Glove award in Monte-Carlo in 1987 for his acrobatic skills in the Arnaoutov Russian Cradle Act, a discipline created in 1936 by his father and now practised around the world. In 1990, Dmitrii became the Flying Man when he introduced the aerial solo straps genre to America. He created this act in the Moscow Circus and toured the world with Cirque du Soleil's *Nouvelle Expérience* show. Currently, Dmitrii shares his knowledge as a trainer in different circus schools. He previously worked as a coach and expert for various Cirque du Soleil productions.

I met Dmitrii when I was a teenager; we were training in the same venue in Quebec City. Eventually, we performed for the same events, at times travelling together. He was 35 years older than me but had a fitter body than the 20-year-old male star acrobats. With his thick but charming Russian accent, he gave me advice that was rarely in tune with that of my coaches at the time.

Dmitrii was a complete misfit in our environment for several reasons: His approach to training and coaching was utterly counter-intuitive to my knowledge at the time. He was doing endless repetitions with lower difficulty elements, which did not seem productive. He chose a slower progression, and I was used to the risk-taking approach that dominated the company I was evolving with. Although the adrenaline effect was a daily drug for the young acrobats we were, I witnessed many serious accidents and injuries during these years. Several of my colleagues sustained severe lesions. Dmitrii and his wife Irina, also an acrobat already in her forties, did not seem to suffer any real pain, oddly enough. Every time he practised, he behaved as if onstage; looking up gracefully, keeping his impressive posture well after stepping back on the ground, as if he had cameras pointed at him. Dmitrii did everything to perfection even if that meant keeping his little finger up towards an imaginary audience. He practised under real conditions, which was a rule I adopted for myself. Practising as if there was an audience became the respect I pay to my body and Art. I know what I'm doing creates damage to my body. Therefore, every single time I rise in the air or go on my hands, I give my very best aesthetically, artistically, technically. Even if no one is watching, I never neglect the details. As a result, they became part of me.

Although using perfect technique decreases damage on your joints, every time you practice a trick, your expiration date comes nearer.

Make every single second of your training worthy.

I observed Dmitrii's attention to details for many years. He ate meticulously. When we were touring on a bus, while other acrobats would buy snacks during a highway pit stop on that never-ending ride between Toronto and Quebec City, Dmitrii used the full break to stretch and walk. He is the only artist I've shared a stage with who had a warm-up routine as long as mine, not to mention the after-show cool-down session. He made no exceptions. I was accustomed to spending the first hour or two alone backstage before anyone showed up: no longer when he was on the same show.

Well into his fifties, Dmitrii was still performing as a soloist, bare-chested, flying on one arm, doing the splits. I was genuinely impressed by what leads someone to that perfect condition at that age. What struck me was that he always seemed to work with enthusiasm; his training seemed somehow spiritual to him. He exuded a zen discipline even when encountering a difficult session. When anybody else would have been visibly annoyed, he lost his smile but kept his focus and worked on the problem endlessly if needed.

Dmitrii is the incarnation of consistency and congruency, spread over five decades. In my research on the ageing process focusing on athletes, I've interviewed different world-class physical performers who broke the age rule in their field, but Dmitrii's answers deserved a whole chapter.

INTERVIEW FOR PHYSICAL PERFORMER AGAINST THE CLOCK PROJECT

At the time of this writing, Dmitrii is 70 years old. He began working professionally at the age of eight in the Moscow Circus, following his parent's footsteps and joining them in their Russian Cradle Act as a flyer. He actively pursued his professional circus career as an artist until the age of 60, still flying in his aerial straps.

He believes he reached his physical peak at the age of 30 and artistically at 45.

In the Soviet Union, Dmitrii spent the entire day training at the circus, from morning until performance time.

'I would usually spend about an hour on a specific apparatus and the rest of the time doing flexibility and conditioning. Most exercises were circus specific. For example, we would not just do a push-up; we would do a handstand push-up. We wouldn't do a simple squat; we would put another acrobat on our shoulders and then do a squat. Wherever there was space, we would all train, and everyone was welcome in the circus ring'.

Dmitrii spent four days a week training five hours a day on top of the six-days-a-week performance regimen until his thirties. When he started a family, he reduced his training schedule drastically and reassessed his program.

Most artists practising aerial acrobatics experience shoulder injuries—overuse due to repetitive motion results in the destruction of their ligaments and tendons. The damage seems to now happen at an even younger age; many artists have not yet finished their circus school education when they have their first shoulder surgery. I think the acrobatic level is rising and the body preparation is not keeping up at the same pace. I see several young artists unaware that they are self-sabotaging. It would be too easy to attribute this to the social media epidemy and the rise of immediate success and need for attention, although there might be some truth there. In our field, instant success is an illusion. Simple tricks sometimes take ten years to learn to be performed safely and accurately. Dmitrii said he never experienced any major injuries in his career. He attributes this *luck* to a proper warm-up, keeping himself in constant working physical shape, and some smart decisions!

He humbly says: 'Performers get injured in new tricks with the lack of proper practice beforehand. I always made sure to practice every trick safely and repeatedly, before including it in a performance. Good technique always goes a long way'.

I think performers are often misled by their ego, making bad decisions resulting in their physical decline or, in some case, dramatic falls. What seems to have helped Dmitrii is uncommon wisdom in his performing choices. 'I was always trying to keep a realistic balance between my desires and actual physical abilities,' he said. He made sure his repertoire of movements would be manageable for a career length. It sounds logical, but it is challenging psychologically not to perform movements we know we can show off to the world—but choose not to—because it's not sustainable. Learning to make the right decision to save your physique, choosing not to publicly display skills you work for your whole life, requires remarkable self-assurance.

The ratio of practising versus injury prevention changed with time. As a young athlete, Dmitrii did not allocate any time to injury prevention but mostly strength training. With time and wisdom, his training eventually shifted to 80% injury prevention and 20% practice.

When I asked Dmitrii about the most significant challenge he faced as an ageing performer, he confessed that he only developed physical hurdles after the age of 50.

'Everything became so hard to achieve and so fast to lose'.

His biggest physical challenge with age became the lack of energy and motivation to keep himself in top shape.

'It requires a lot of effort and becomes more and more demanding to maintain an elite physical form'.

After taking a short break from his training regimen, he used to be back on top of his game after a few days; as he aged, the same would require several weeks. That leaves no space for downtime; the price for regaining the losses is too high.

It is difficult to pinpoint the secret to Dmitrii's exceptional longevity in the business. The humble Dmitrii says it might be attributed to good genes or pure luck, but he admits that his self-care and self-respect must have played a role. 'Your body is a horse that rides you through life; you must love and respect it if you want to go far. You must be its friend, not its enemy,' he so eloquently says.

PART 3

Career

Chapter 11

My day as an athlete

———————————

Coherence defines performance,
using the smallest detail for improvement.

My schedule is a roller coaster, continually hopping from one plane to another, changing time zones, country, lifestyle, diet. The chaos exists within a rigorous discipline that I slightly adjust to the daily reality.

I may work in a theatre where I perform every night at 8 p.m. for months. Other times, I train for weeks for a one-time TV show shooting in the morning, meaning I have to readjust my peak performance energy to mornings—the body performs best at a trained time of day, and you can acclimatise it by repetitions. I have precise routines for many schedules, and I adapt to the new priorities, keeping planning as strict as possible.

'How you spend your days is how you spend your life'.

These words of Annie Dillard resonate with me. To achieve anything meaningful, you must go through repetitive actions, which become the main players that constitute your life. A schedule puts order in the mess of existence, and ultimately, the portrait of your entire project we call life. You may need to be the incarnation of discipline, but make sure when you look back on the last 1,000 days, you willingly chose each day. It's easy to get caught up in a pattern that no longer serves us. To avoid this, ask the following question every single day: Is there anything you are doing because you are stuck in a recurrent scheme for which you can no longer find the why? Or is every action of your day still coherent with the purpose?

On a typical day, when not travelling or performing, I like to get up before the sun. Not for its romantic appeal but for the benefit I get from natural lights for sleeping patterns and quality. I keep external stimuli non-existent; i.e. no phone or computer use.

First, I meditate and write down my short-, medium-, and long-term goals. I do that daily, although most of it is a repetition of the previous day. They need to be precise and fresh in my mind.

If I have a disastrous day, it will be easier to remember the reasons I'm imposing that upon myself. In addition to the recurring goals, every morning, I define what I need to focus on each day.

I then boil fresh ginger in a huge pot. That will be the only thing I ingest for the next two hours. I love to listen to classical music in the early hours, especially during my *Physical Poetry* body preparation—a precise technique set up in a continuous flow of movement. It is designed to rebalance my body, fixing any minor injuries from the previous training day. I work on muscular tension and release joints that are becoming inflamed. I prepare every single part of my body for the new day of training, reducing the risks of injury as much as possible. That 'body wake-up' lasts from 40 to 60 minutes on average.

Afterwards, I usually have a 60-minute cardio session. I choose low-impact interval training such as elliptical, inclined fast walking, or swimming, so I don't add extra stress on my joints.

I have breakfast, the very same thing I've had every morning for the last decade, with slight changes. I weigh the portions of everything I eat; this is not an eating disorder but pure practicality to be precise with my diet.

A six to eight egg-white omelette with cacao and stevia, one apple, and four walnuts, sometimes substituted by 60 grams (2 ounces) of avocado. Almond milk cappuccino: I make my milk with 100% natural almond powder pre-ground and ready to be mixed with water. One scoop of hydrolysed collagen powder from pasture-raised cows without added hormones.

After breakfast and a short email and business assessment, I attack my most valuable chunk of training. I keep the most difficult part for when I have more energy and focus—mornings. Strength, endurance, joint stability, and active flexibility program are on the daily menu—three hours of the most substantial part of my training day. I follow the plan; I push and don't question. I also go through all the basics; most are for my hand-balancing skills and require more repetition than anything else in my field. I consider hand-balancing as classical dance performed upside down. It's the purest form of acrobatic art to me. The absolute perfection of lines and technique will let me achieve the most difficult movements. I approach this discipline with the utmost sense of analysis. I have video recorded every session for as far back as I can remember. I correct the slightest angle, imperfection, visual detail that I can improve for technical and aesthetic purposes.

To make my days more productive, knowing I have to go through these repetitions for hours daily, I usually learn something new by listening to a podcast or audiobook. I like to perfect one of the languages I speak or learn a new one. I may listen to medical courses in neuroscience or a thought-provoking memoir by an inspiring artist. I want to be challenged in my thinking processes. I avoid the headlines or anything that would poison my day and be short-lived. Will knowing this information matter in five years? With the news and its fear-based nature, in 95% of cases, the answer is no. I direct my time towards what remains alive— the tangible. This philosophy of life is in line with every choice I make. I look at the longer perspective: what I grow today should remain valid in 10 years or be a foundation for something I'll keep building in the future. That goes for my business and personal relationships as well as the things I put in my brain when I have a 10-minute break.

Lunch consists of fresh vegetables and wild-caught fish, mainly in huge, colourful salads. I won't eat half-seated by the kitchen counter; my meals are a ritual. Even when eating alone, I take time to make an aesthetically pleasing meal for myself. I love beauty; that must apply to the food in front of me too. I set the table and take time to eat. I avoid sugar, but the occasional fruit or raw cacao with stevia and almond milk, resulting in a chocolate mousse, are my sweet bites of excellence. I eat three healthy meals per day with no snacks. Snacking adds unwanted calories and, most of the time, they are mediocre types of food: pre-packed bars, starches, salty, and sugary items.

Having a sweet tooth is an understatement for me. Fruits make my brain scream with joy; I'd nibble on them all day long. I noticed I felt tired about 40 minutes after eating one or two fruits alone, which makes me want to retire for good when thinking of another training session. After wearing a glucose sensor for 14 days—a little device with a small needle implanted in your skin that, paired with a smartphone, tracks your blood sugar—I found that eating a big apple alone would send my blood sugar through the roof. That glucose level then crashes, creating this unexplained lethargic feeling. That is what I had suspected, but seeing the graph made me decrease my fruit consumption and always pair them with lipids or proteins unless I want to become a professional couch potato.

At the beginning of my thirties, I started to eat considerably more fats and fewer proteins for anti-ageing and anti-inflammatory reasons. Adding a few more raw nuts or avocado pieces and smaller portions of organic chicken or fish made the ratio of macronutrients shift considerably.

I am very diligent about the amount of protein I consume. Every calorie is chosen to nourish me properly. This way, I eat satiating meals without too many calories that would make it impossible for me to maintain a lightweight frame. I know the sweet spot for me to stay lean and keep my muscle mass. Under-eating will cause losses in muscle mass, which is neither functional nor attractive.

After lunch, I meditate shortly again. This way, I press the reset button and gather the necessary spirit for the afternoon session. My energy levels are nowhere near where they were in the morning. I have less resistance to pain, and I am psychologically weaker; therefore, I fail a lot earlier. I dedicate the afternoon session to creation, incorporating a more artistic training—aerial exploration, movements research, new ideas I want to translate into my Art. One might find me waving uncontrollably through the air whilst holding myself by one foot as an experiment. That's the moment I cherish having my personal creation studio for the sake of not being locked up in a mental institute by concerned colleagues. I sometimes have to use this time to develop and perfect an upcoming piece. It's physically less demanding and creatively motivating: my treat of the day.

I eat dinner early. It is more or less a copy of lunch: seafood, vegetables, and moderate fruit consumption. I am a coffee lover, and although I know it can disrupt sleep quality, I do not experience any insomnia. I literally pass out in bed at night. Coffee is my vice and the conclusion to every single meal. Strong Italian espresso is the way to go for me.

I save work for the evenings, once I'm entirely out of my creative space. I condense anything business-related, managing a worldwide career, into a two-hour chunk. I am much more efficient than if I answer sporadically during the day, throwing me in and out of my mindset. Once I shut myself into the office and delve into business mode, I go through a day of work in a few hours. Mono-focussing is an essential tool. Multi-tasking is a myth to make people with short attention spans feel better about themselves. You can't be precise and efficient without allowing uncompromised attention to one matter at a time. Plus, the time needed to shift attention and dive into an issue is lost when surfing between them.

I love to read books at night, mainly non-fiction and philosophy, where I find inspiration, oddly enough, for my choreographies and visual pieces. I recently reconnected with a lost decade of novels. I somehow translate ideas into images while reading. I never watch TV and keep my procrastination level on social networks to a minimum. I hate to have lost 25 minutes doing nothing for myself. I restrict my usage of social networks to active posting. I do not passively 'consume' other people's lives online. I'm too busy with mine.

I usually have a bath with magnesium before bed to relax my muscles and give them a chance to recover. When I'm diligent with cold therapy and don't skip the cold bath, I get the best night's sleep. If I don't have to fly somewhere for a performance, I'll repeat this for three days in a row. I then have a lighter day, only dedicated to creativity, and I repeat a three-day chunk before finally taking a full day off. I do not function according to the days of the week; a Wednesday is like a Sunday to me. I set the rules.

These repetitive days are dedicated to my long-term goal: my vocation.

Chapter 12

My day as an artist

Travel and show days: no off season.

PHOTOGRAPHY: LAZARINA KANOROVA

My core market consists of high-end events. Performing for the select few is like being on call 365 days a year. There is no off season when the best opportunity of a career may present itself 48 hours beforehand.

Travelling and show days are completely different animals.

I often fly overseas for a performance. To be in good condition, I ask my client to arrange my arrival a day before rehearsals for acclimatisation. It's not always possible as sometimes I'm performing in India on Monday, Italy on Tuesday, and Brazil on Thursday. But if my schedule allows, it's a prerequisite.

Even now, it is something I have to explain to collaborators. Clients may ignore that the care we give to our body will result in the quality of the show they are paying for—that the few minutes of spectacle exists due to a no-exception lifestyle. There won't be an exceptional performance without exceptional working conditions.

A few years ago, I was performing solo to launch a Cirque du Soleil show on behalf of the company in Sao Paulo, Brazil. Their client asked me if I could fly from Europe, and on arrival, go directly to the TV venue where the press conference was taking place. Then proceed to full rehearsal, including acrobatics and contortions for their camera test. And the next day at 10 a.m.— implying a wake-up call at 4 a.m. for my preparation—perform for their national TV spot and hop on the next plane back to Europe. To this day, I remain perplexed when addressed this way. Between two deep breaths, I remind myself we have to educate our audience and our clients about the specifics of our field. I do take time to explain the reasons why I need to rest after an overseas trip, why sleep is critical for a safe and successful performance and not just a starlet's fancy request. I explain that I can't perform to perfection and am more prone to injury after a long flight. I need proper lighting and stage rehearsals to feel safe and work accurately, and the quality and time of performance directly influence the visual result they'll use to promote a mega-show touring for 10 weeks, countrywide. It is exhausting to repeatedly go through such basics, but education requires patience. The company itself knows about these important details, but the country provider media company they collaborated with did not connect the dots that what they see onstage is made possible due to extraordinary body conditions.

Clients often say, 'We won't see the difference if you aren't perfect'. I spent my life running after perfection and dedicated every minute to get as close to it as possible whilst onstage. I have too much respect for myself and my Art not to stick to my rules. I didn't choose this life to settle for less than my very best potentiality. An audience will never know your potential unless you show them. Don't bother explaining the whys later; you have one chance to prove your point, and it happens during the few minutes you are in the spotlights. When you are the one onstage, alone, insist on putting in the extra effort, relentlessly.

Before travelling, every detail such as stage space, timing, audience quantity, and quality (because the quality of an audience does exist), dressing room (before, during, and after the show), press and speeches must be planned meticulously.

If the trip involves a shift in time zones, sleep before travelling is key. Do not buy into the false assumption that being tired before the flight will make you fall asleep on the plane and adapt to your new time zone more quickly. Unfortunately, the body clock doesn't function that way. Your body will adapt easily to your new time zone if rested and its capacity of adaptation are fit.

Being on a plane for 12 hours is literally breathing in a virus box. You'd better have a robust immune system. For decades, I made it a habit to clean my seat, tray, and hands repeatedly during the flight, looking like an insane person. I get up every hour to do squats in the aisle. It is an easy and efficient exercise to maintain blood flow. I hide in common areas to exercise and stretch while passengers are sleeping. I do not consume alcohol; you're already subject to dehydration on an aircraft due to the low level of moisture and alcohol will worsen it. I drink a lot of water, and I avoid the salty food they serve by bringing my own.

When I arrive at my destination, I want to see where I'll be performing and be aware of any possible technical strains on my team that I may have missed during negotiation. How far away from the stage is my dressing room? Is there a warm area to stay and lie down next to the stage before stepping on? Will I look at the audience at the same eye level, or are they seated higher or lower than I am? In which case, I'd readjust the angles of some movements slightly to give them a better view when possible. I like to feel the stage and its energy and let it grow in my mind overnight. The performance space needs to become part of the show.

I check the level of the stage floor since any possible unevenness compromises my balancing capabilities. Some clients seem to think that performers are inhuman and can effortlessly compensate a 10-degree shift with the strength of a finger. I needed to add this to my contract: levelled stage means zero degrees denivelation or I fall.

I then look up to the ceiling to inspect the hanging specificities needed for my aerial acts—if anything needs to be modified, the technical team will have the night to make the changes before the morning's rehearsals.

Things rarely go as planned, so I make space for problems in the schedule. By expecting issues, I'm rarely short of solutions.

As soon as I check into my hotel, I have a cardio session even if it's bedtime. I use a cold bath and saunas, if available, to get rid of water retention and prepare my muscles for the next day's rehearsal. I sleep as long as possible.

EQUIPMENT AND INSTALLATION

My trusted certified technician and I install the aerial gear, which allows me to 'magically' fly up and down. I inspect every single piece of my lightweight and compact rigging equipment. It consists of pulleys, shackles, swivels, and quick links. I choose the visually less disturbing option, instead of the default size, and each item has a working load sufficient for the dynamic factor I generate while in movement, including the security factor required. The smallest piece of equipment I use to secure my life is a nano swivel with a working load of three kilonewtons (674 pounds) and a breaking load of 23 kilonewtons (5,170 pounds). That means I could binge on chocolate cake for a lifetime and still be within a secure range. Despite all the professional security checks done at the venue, I always double-check everything I attach in the air. Since I wasn't there when the place was built, if something happens to one of the beams or hooks, I'm always secured to a second one.

INSTALLATION AND SECURITY POLICY

For years, I installed the aerial acrobatic equipment myself; depending on the venue policies, there might be a local operator to help. Nowadays, I travel with my trusted technician, and even though I can rely on him entirely, I prefer to supervise the process. When human lives are at risk, our ego must take a step back, and more verification is always better. A good technician will respect and agree with this. If he or she feels insulted by my presence, they are probably not the right person for the job. A professional rigger will be happy to answer the artist's every question about his or her security. A good technician will always remain calm and never rush the process, even under pressure. Most accidents happen due to a tiny detail neglected. I prefer to lose time verifying equipment. I also demand to be double-checked and challenged in my security choices.

As an aerial performer, *you* are responsible for your safety. In the mind of others, we are often regarded as superhumans, as if what they see had magically appeared in our life, forgetting we can only do these stunts when all conditions are present. That explains why I sometimes witness staff walking under me when I am rehearsing in the air or a light technician provoking a full black-out in the room while I'm balancing on one foot atop a high stick. How am I supposed to balance then? Do not assume others know the level of difficulty of your skills and the decades behind each movement. Sadly, accidents happen—horrific accidents happen—and each time we hear or read in the newspaper, 'this is incomprehensible; he/she was an experienced acrobat', the truth is, we don't fly. We play with the laws of gravity, and one speck of dust may change the physics.

I never cut corners on safety. I never allow laziness even if I haven't slept in 48 hours. If I suspect the slightest damage to a piece of equipment, which might still be fit to work nonetheless, I substitute it immediately. I inspect my equipment before every use, and I expect my technician to do the same. Security standards are never too high.

REHEARSALS AND SHOW DAY

As much as I'd prefer to have more days of preparation, there are time constraints. I sometimes rehearse for hours right before the show, which isn't ideal since I should be resting and only exercising lightly.

I reach the performing venue early to warm up. When rehearsals and the show occur on the same day, during light and audio tests, I'll exclude some specific movements requiring extensive preparation or that are more traumatic to the body.

I then sit with the lighting designer to go through every cue we previously set and make changes, if needed. After the technical rehearsals, I do the full act under real conditions. That includes light, music, and introduction by a host if any. I want to know how many steps I need to take before reaching the centre stage, where I start my performance, how many seconds it requires. This rehearsal should be perfect and the show precisely the same, down to the smallest detail. Too often, details are neglected and put into the wishful thinking that it will go as planned. You don't want an artistic masterpiece to become referred to as the malfunction in the evening. I prefer to let go of magical expectations and do the extra work, even if the team around me is rolling their eyes.

FEEDING BODY AND MIND

Three hours before showtime, I start my make-up and hair preparation right after a healthy meal is delivered to my dressing room. Unlike some other performers, I do eat before a show, but I leave three hours between a meal and a performance. Easy to digest, high-density food that won't occupy space in my stomach is best. It's near torture to contort with a full stomach, and the fear of not keeping it in when spinning upside down, well, is real.

When I'm all made up for the show, I dive into my last 90-minute focus bubble. Knowing that most of the time, unexpected things happen, my concentration needs to be nearly impossible to disrupt. I have a precise and timed schedule of preparation before going onstage, but I always keep some extra time for potential changes or problems.

I worked on reaching a profound level of calm before a show. Adrenaline will keep me sharp; stress can push me to make mistakes. If I am prepared enough, the show will be a moment of bliss and interpretation. If I am short on preparation, it will be a mishmash of conflicted messages and trying to avoid mistakes.

Chapter 13

Body image

Reaching 7% body fat for athletic needs.

PHOTOGRAPHY: DAVID CANNON

I've always been hesitant to talk about weight, my diet, and body image publicly. It's a delicate subject that can quickly lead to misinterpretation. During my teenage years, I was surrounded by several, sometimes life-threatening, cases of eating disorders. I am sensitive to the vulnerability of young women—and increasingly young men—especially those practising a sport or art that requires extreme leanness or where physical appearance plays a role. If you have a poor relationship with food or self-image, I stress the importance of seeking help as soon as possible. The damage done by anorexia, bulimia, or other eating disorders can be fatal and is *always* destructive. A few upsides may blind you at first: being praised for a sudden loss of weight, a rewarding feeling of control, for instance. However, these upsides will vanish and turn into a nightmare if untreated.

Before I share my story, I have to clarify that I do not encourage any unhealthy behaviour. My approach to body image may sound rigid but is purely practical and functional: sports-oriented. I would lie if I said there isn't a desire to reach a precise aesthetic in this consideration. However, there is no beauty in a malnourished body. Eating disorders are not dieting gone wrong; they are a disease to address seriously. It is, unfortunately, often overlooked in those who do not show signs of extreme thinness. In these frequent cases, however, distress is still present. One does not need to be underweight to suffer and put his or her health at risk. The disorder starts inside, not outside.

BODY CHANGES

I was always an extremely skinny child. My grandmother would give me pocket money if I put on weight; my mother would hide butter in my sandwiches between slices of meat. I had a good appetite, but it was just the way I was built. I looked like a stick, having grown only in length and not in width. My thinness became fuel for bullies. Luckily, I quickly shut them up with my remarkable athletic performances at school; it helps when the 'toothpick' runs faster and does more pull-ups than the bully.

My journey in the show business world started at such a young age, and I quickly gained the reputation of being the 'skinny girl' in the business. It somehow defined me onstage and offstage. Without being aware of it, I've built part of my identity on this simple fact. People praised me for my physique, and my light weight was useful for several circus disciplines for which I needed to be carried by colleagues. In these cases, weight becomes a regular topic. 'What's your weight?' before 'What's your name?' is not uncommon.

At 15, I had my first weight-related concern. I was a flyer for a Russian cradle act—two men standing on aerial platforms propelling me into the air while I was executing acrobatic movements. A new girl joined the company, and she was significantly shorter than me, therefore lighter. Although I was acrobatically skilled and worked harder than everyone else, I was left out of a few movements where the weight difference was in her favour. It's the first time of my life I considered eating less. It was simple rational thinking: by losing weight, I'd fly higher and be able to enhance my skills. I've always done everything that was in my power to improve; nothing was going to stop me, especially not something as fixable as weight, I thought. Eventually, however, my long legs became an element to underline. With the coach, we explored an acrobatic vocabulary to emphasise my attributes instead of trying to reach a weight that was not viable, only to fly higher.

Years later, at 17 years old, I suddenly put on 15% of my mass in three months. I was still lean but not the skinny girl anymore. Everyone seemed to notice, and I was receiving teasing comments from co-workers and family. Both girls in the company with whom I was partnering started to have difficulty supporting my weight. Not only my colleagues but also the director began to be involved in finding a solution. I did not fit in my clothes anymore. I was in a panic state. I was ashamed. I had always had everything under control, and that had just changed. The level of judgement I held towards myself was immensely destructive. I knew nothing about nutrition and had always been a sugar addict; it used to be cute to see the skinny girl eat two desserts in a row.

Faced with this new physical challenge, I reacted incorrectly. I tried to skip meals, got overly hungry after training, and ate the wrong food continuously. My eating—or trying not to eat—became exclusively snacking, which made things worse. I looked into diet pills, unhealthy diet bars advertised as 'meal replacements', but I kept putting on weight. This issue required patience, which I did not possess at 17 years old. I had to wear my little white unitard and walk out onstage—in front of an audience, in front of colleagues, in front of myself. This sudden increase in weight made it difficult to climb up and do my usual performance. For the first time in my life, I did not want to be in the spotlight. Every day, I felt I needed to come up with an immediate solution, which was obviously the wrong mindset. By wanting to fix the weight issue, I became obsessed with the matter, and it consumed all my psychological space.

I eventually regained control over my weight, but the experience terrified me. In hindsight, I am grateful for that uncomfortable period of my life since it started my journey of health and nutrition. I began studying nutrition, glucose regulation, and hormonal response. I learned how many calories and the exact number of macronutrients every meal contained. I will use this knowledge for my whole life. I know the correct balance to lose weight, gain muscle, etc. The entire path has been empowering.

As a result, I became healthier, rarely got sick, was less prone to infections. From an external viewpoint, I had a toned, healthy body. I pursued my career for several years on a rather healthy diet, but I still wasn't happy about the way I looked. I am naturally thin and have difficulty growing muscle; therefore, I look more like the girl next door and not an elite athlete. The situation wasn't ideal, and I rarely felt satiated. In 2010, I decided that good wasn't enough. There was no point settling for less than perfect. I wanted to push my body to the next level.

I saw room to improve my lines and form to emphasise my style. With the help of a body-building coach, I've unlearned some of my eating habits. Some of it was the opposite of what I had been convinced was the only truth for years. My perfect diet was somewhere in the middle, but I committed to fully trusting this person, which was the only way to address this significant change for me at the time. I've fine-tuned my diet down to the smallest detail. I reduced the number of calories to the bare minimum for having enough energy to feed my muscles. I raised my protein consumption to 40%-50% of my total daily consumption. I eliminated soy—known to be an endocrine disruptor—and my habit of overly consuming fruits to reduce the ratio of carbohydrates in my diet. I added fasted cardio sessions daily, upping the energy burn. I stopped compromising on my sleeping habits, and I stopped eating out. I prepared every meal and weighed my food. I had the freedom to choose what I commit to—anything that wasn't in line with this fell to the bottom of my priority list. I erased most forms of social life; I was on a mission. I took consistency to a new level. It was thrilling to witness.

I lost body fat quickly. I became so lean I could see the veins even on my upper abdomen. My legs seemed more muscular and defined, although they were thinner. I focussed my days exclusively on my training and self-care. I became stronger and technically more precise than ever. I felt like I was flying when on my hands. I dedicated five months to get into the best functional shape I could ever be. The results showed. In March 2010, I carried around 14%-16% body fat; five months later, I was a little bit below 6%. I eventually settled at about 7%.

Was it difficult? Of course! But failing my goal and having to step onstage, not looking and feeling the way I had projected was not an alternative. There was no backup plan in my head.

Losing body fat when you are already lean must be done very specifically. The leaner you are, the harder it becomes as your body rebels. It wants to keep fat for survival and childbearing as a woman.

THE DOWNSIDES

During the seven years I kept my body fat around 7%, I was regularly having blood drawn to make sure I wasn't causing damage to my health. I supplemented carefully, but on a hormonal level, a woman's body doesn't like to be that lean. I felt my regenerative capabilities were a little impaired, probably due to the insufficient production of some female hormones.

My skin wasn't as radiant as it could be. The gauntness of my face made me look old. It is not the best choice for a purely aesthetic point of view. I didn't look my best, and I was aware of it, but I did not see it as a principal concern.

The most disturbing side effects were not physical though. What was astounding was the lack of diplomacy directed towards me. Many felt compelled to comment on my body or my size, sometimes in a very negative way and without my invitation. If someone is overweight, we go through mental contortions to avoid the subject or find a diplomatic answer to the 'Do I look fat?' question. As a skinny person, constant attacks and unsolicited comments abound:

'Come on! You are too skinny. You can have dessert!'

'You diet too much'.

'You would look better with more weight'.

'How much do you weigh?'

Not to mention the constant alluding to me being sick and having a disorder.

These comments came regularly from colleagues, acquaintances, flight attendants—as a free, unsolicited add-on whilst serving me a meal, the clerk selling me clothes in a boutique, and random strangers on the street. If you want to stand out, you'll disturb; although you think you threaten no one, you do! You need to become impermeable to what others think of you. The most important person to please remains yourself.

Chapter 14

Your real value

Success is not always about winning,
and sometimes, failure is the catalyst.

I've always been extremely results-oriented. Even as a child, I didn't value my efforts or improvements—only the outcomes—a dangerous pattern to design for oneself. I wanted to be the best. I did not care if others noticed I was, but I needed to see the results for myself. Today, the little eight-year-old who did not accept a single mistake in her math exams has evolved, but I still must remind myself where my real value resides.

In 2012, I was already a well-established artist with an international reputation. My career was going full-steam, and I had created a market for myself with the creative freedom I was yearning. I can humbly say I had a reason to be proud of what I had achieved. I had already won several of the most important international competitions in my field. And I had done so independently of any institutions, always representing my sole name and brand. Part of me wouldn't be satisfied until I did the last big competition: Le Festival International du Cirque de Monte-Carlo. Created in 1974 by H.S.H. Prince Rainier III of Monaco, the International Circus Festival of Monte-Carlo has become the largest and most prestigious circus event in the world. Organised and presided over by H.S.H. Princess Stéphanie of Monaco, a selection of the best international acts is presented each year at the festival, which is broadcast around the globe.

This show is famous for bringing together numerous circus troupes who risk their lives before an audience with the most incredible acrobatics on earth. Amongst more than 200 artists from 22 countries, I was the only soloist invited to present two different acts in the program. My style was much more contemporary: *Physical Poetry* communicates a message through physical languages; the acrobatics are a vehicle, not an end. Although I had worked for years at dissociating myself from the 'circus' world, a part of me was longing for this once-in-a-lifetime occasion.

I knew this platform might not be the one to highlight my style, but I still had high expectations. I was counting on adding that last missing prize to my international collection of accolades. I prepared for months until the time had come to step into the ring. From the start, something was off. Between the lions and the large acrobat troupes occupying the big-top, my performances were not particularly standing out on this stage. I doubted myself. I felt invisible. I was not at the best of my capabilities, feeling I was a misfit. I won a special prize, presented by Patrick Hourdequin—Prix de l' Association Monégasque des Amis du Cirque—for which I am thankful, but the big award never came. I did not win a medal.

Up to that point, I thought my self-worth was unshakeable, but this episode made me question my value not only as an artist but also as a person. Why was I putting so much energy into this? It's probably one of the downsides of being so single-focussed; my whole life used to gravitate around one professional project. I could rationalise the entire episode. I was aware it was not the market I was even interested in for my future. Nevertheless, that mediocre result was engraved on my pedigree now. It portrayed the destruction of a little girl's dream, as ludicrous as it may sound today.

I carried on with my growing career, barely hurt by this failure from the outside. I shone on many TV shows that year and kept developing new pieces of *Physical Poetry*, in line with my future.

Success is not always winning. Success is moving forward, and sometimes, failure is the catalyst.

I now see this defeat as a very successful chapter of my career since it put a definitive mark on my circus upbringing. I was finally at peace with turning my back on my past, unapologetically wearing the professional identity I had fought to build. I could now dedicate myself to the market I had developed. More importantly, I was coherent with the direction I was going, regardless of pride or little girl's dreams. My *Physical Poetry* was not fit for the traditional circus. It was a blessing that the jury and organization of the most celebrated circus festival on earth shut that door on me. They helped me realise my old dreams were obsolete.

In October of the same year, only eight months after the episode that had shaken my ego, The Ritz-Carlton Montreal hosted an elegant gala to celebrate the hotel's 100th anniversary. For the occasion, Cirque du Soleil was commissioned to deliver a tailor-made show. I was chosen to perform as the principal soloist on behalf of the company that night. The Ritz's luxurious Royal Suite was inaugurated by Their Serene Highnesses Prince Albert II and Princess Charlene of Monaco, who had witnessed from the first row my 'failure' onstage in Monaco. That night, they came to congratulate me personally and said it would be an honour to have me at Le Festival International du Cirque de Monte-Carlo. I smiled, grateful for their kindness. I couldn't help picturing myself as a different piece of the same chessboard.

By letting an external system influence your value, you hand over a part of your identity to others. Seen that way, I'm ashamed, not of my failure this time, but of my reaction to it.

SET YOUR WORTH BUT LIVE UP TO IT

You set your worth as a professional being, but then you must live up to the price tag. No one should ever feel entitled. I am aware of being one of—if not *the* most—expensive artists in the business, but it comes with a responsibility. You must make sure clients and audiences have nothing to complain about. By demanding excellence, you have to remain beyond reproach and your craft always beyond expectation. You must be in perfect shape every day of the year. You need to be immaculate not only during the show but also in rehearsals.

The whole adventure of hiring an artist must be the answer to the price. A client is not only paying the fee for your performance but is trusting you with their most important clients. They partially put their reputation in your hands. The offstage experience must equal the level you show onstage. Take every single step of the process as if it was the most crucial task of your life. The negotiation and contractual agreement, the moment you are being picked up at the airport, the set-up of your equipment, the way you address the technical team, the moment you walk offstage after your performance. Everything must be sharp. A client or the audience should never see you unbalanced. Your stage excellence must translate into backstage class and perfection. Only then can you say you are professional.

Knowing some of the audience members might recognise me, I don't have drinks in a hotel lobby after the show.

It matters.

I politely decline food if I have to be near the audience after I performed, even if starving. I ask my meal to be served in my dressing room instead. The idea of the ethereal flying princess shall remain as is, without a piece of salad between her teeth.

Hold yourself to high ethical standards. Define and respect your contract and timing by the book. It's ethical to refuse to work at a lower price or perform for events that are not of the right calibre, even if clients can pay the fee. My only exception to that rule is one charity a year I perform for complimentarily. To work in an elite market, the clients you are after will not appreciate knowing you perform in cheap or common events. Your price tag is also a quality tag. To belong to a high-end environment, you must prove your point through your actions.

Things never go as planned. Every now and then, you might end up working in a mediocre environment where professionals are acting like amateurs. It happens even in the highest spheres. And unfortunately, it's contagious: the rotten apple analogy is not a myth.

In such conditions, fly above. Make sure you never lower your standards, especially towards yourself. Doing so would be a disrespect to your craft. Even if you perform on a non-professional stage with barely any audience, always aim to deliver your best performance. If no one is watching, do it for yourself and walk off-stage proudly. I've seen so many artists skip their preparation steps because the audience is non-VIP or failing to correct an artistic issue in their act before the last show of a hundred, thinking no one will notice. In every situation, perform as if it was the opportunity of a lifetime or the last of your career. And in this business, it might as well be.

Chapter 15

Work on your skills, not just your flaws

Fix your weak links and don't let others define you.

If you are critical of yourself, you might give too much space or energy to your imperfections. Don't build your practice and identity by endlessly focussing on your flaws. Use as much time as possible to work on your skills, on what you excel at, improving them further, becoming the one-in-a-million.

However, if you notice you are not working full speed due to a flaw, stop everything else and fix it, even if it takes a year. It's much more efficient to do so intensely rather than drag a handicap for years, with the excuse of not having time. Start by fixing your weak links instead of using precious time working at a decreased pace. You always lose at the game of camouflaging flaws or trying to hide personal stains from others. Sometimes that's the detail that keeps you from flying to the moon.

With your craft, never compromise on quality—contentment is not enough. Reach beyond your best, and then push a little more, continuously.

DON'T LET *THEM* DEFINE *YOU*

You know your capabilities better than anyone else. Keep that reputation you have towards yourself intact.

I didn't want to become the best in the world; I wanted to design a new universe.

That Sunday morning in 1994, when I entered the circus space in Canada for the first time, my teachers noticed that my physique was perfect for aerial disciplines. I had prerequisites for that field and became successful fast. It was like the place was waiting for me to shine. It's always been so natural that it became unchallenging, even expected. I had long limbs and a short trunk, which is counter-productive in acrobatics and strength movements but perfect for aerial arts. As a result, I was directed towards a graceful slow type of movement, formerly standard for female aerialists. I didn't enjoy that type of performance as I found the long-legged contortionists posing in the air rather boring. As soon as I stopped flying in duo and became a soloist on the aerial hoop in 2002, I defined my style as an uncommonly dynamic one. Inspired by my childhood friend and colleague Marie-Michelle, who, unlike me, had a very compact and powerful body, I developed my language at a different speed.

The frequent unsolicited comments during my years of learning this new discipline were that I had to slow down: they couldn't see my movements correctly at the pace I was turning. I had to leave time for the audience to admire my lines. This advice represented the polar opposite of what I was working on. These people—some highly recognised professionals I have esteem for—had that visual input engraved in their mind. They didn't know better; their perception was restricted to what they had always seen.

Innovators never become such by chance; they are a special breed with different thinking to start with.

Do you want to make a difference? Start by being an independent thinker. For this to happen, there is no space for comparison. As soon as you compare, you direct your attention to something or someone else. You risk losing your edge, your focus, and the ability to think individually. Inevitably you become limited to someone else's dreams and limitations.

During my two first years of solo practice, I had not yet developed the speed to create the image feeding my purpose. I imagined a violent but passionate tango with my metal companion, the hoop, that would seem to come to life, a choreographed battle between him and I, twirling breathlessly at 10 metres in the air. I had a piece of original music composed for this act—original music would then become one of my trademarks. It was rhythmic and featured the lamenting chanting of a man. It would have been easier to do what I was good at and what the audience was used to receiving—the standard elegant and soft aerial contortionist. I would have owned a professional act earlier and could have worked as a soloist earlier. I preferred to put more time into it, more blood, more ripped skin. Every day for months, I ended my practice on the verge of throwing up from training my inner ear to bear the intense spinning. Like anything else, fighting dizziness needs to be trained and maintained. I called this first solo creation on the hoop, *Tornado*. This act won the bronze medal at the Festival de Cirque de Demain in Paris in 2007.

> '*From the top of her hoop, the Quebec native Erika Lemay*
> *dishevels her audience while connecting without ever [sic]*
> *weakening the most difficult figures*'.
> — LE FIGARO, FRANCE

> '*The delicate-looking Erika Lemay gave*
> *a strong performance on a hoop*'.
> — THE STAGE, UK

I arrived unexpectedly on the international scene, taking the circus world by storm. I had been flying in duo since the age of 11, a completely different technique. Now alone up there, I was setting new rules on what slender girls could do in the air. The dynamic style by female aerialist is, nowadays, more common.

I've never doubted my skills and my potential in the air; I had something different in mind for myself, and I was fierce in pursuing this idea, letting no one influence my direction. I stayed true to my vision and artistic compass. This episode gave me self-worth; I was succeeding at what I had put my mind to. It was not a courageous move though. I was still in my comfort zone—the aerial space—a far cry from the biggest challenge of my acrobatic career.

15.1

A bigger challenge

———————

Your differences might be tools for your success.

PHOTOGRAPHY: TOOFAN HASHEMI

There was one intention I had kept for myself, maybe out of shame of even thinking of it. I did not know it would leave a profound mark on my career.

My artistic venture started with classical ballet when I was four years old. Although I needed more adrenaline and challenges as a child, I always kept this deep affection for classical dance. Ballet is the most demanding form of art. Technically and artistically speaking, you are invisible unless nearly perfect—a constant run towards utmost excellence. Hand-balancing, as classical dance, is stripped of any technical apparatus. Just a pure human body. Any mistake is noticeable; no second take. When onstage, even now, I feel naked with my veins exposed to the audience, ready to be removed of my right to breathe the stage air. As I was fascinated by the discipline, I started seriously practising by myself around the age of 15. I was still working for the company at the time, and the head coach would not give me a time slot in my training schedule for my hand-balancing.

What for? It didn't serve the purpose of the show, and I didn't have the body of a hand-balancer. That was not my place.

I started at a late age; if I wanted to reach a decent level, I had to hurry up.

I practised after our daily performances when we were on tour. When the lights were off and the cast and crew had left, I stayed at the theatre until much later, repeating the same movements thousands of times, falling and getting back on my feet thousands of times. For the next five or six years and even after I had quit the company, I took every occasion I had to spend time on my hands, sometimes moving the furniture of a tiny hotel room in the middle of the night to practice. I needed to become stronger and better to learn my hand-balancing skills. Knowing the level of difficulty I was aiming for, I voted for no days off, no excuses.

I attended workshops with some of the greatest hand-balancers in the country. I paid for one-on-one classes with a well-known Russian coach visiting Montreal, a bare 300 kilometres (186 miles) from where I lived. It was frustrating as I was an internationally awarded performer, but in this role, I was a novice, back to being a *nobody* again. I had to swallow my pride for what I wanted. The first decade of practice as a hand-balancer is stagnant; it takes so many hours to master only the basics and for your body to adapt to the strain caused by the practice. Since you need to spend six hours daily with your wrist in an unnatural position, some develop stress fractures in their arms or wrist problems that are hard to resolve. Plus, the constant pressure on the neck sometimes leads to herniated cervical disks. I was putting so much work into it. I was slowly developing strength and endurance, first with daily 40 minutes of practice being my maximum to eventually reaching a six-hour daily practice. But some of my necessary skills—the ones you must nail down to earn respect from the international community—were not improving as I wanted. I analysed, worked, worked more.

Maybe they were right; I wasn't made for this. My elbows could barely reach a fully extended position; I always had to compensate while balancing on one hand. My weight naturally fell to the lower side of my palms, towards my wrist, when it needed to remain by the joints of the fingers. I diligently studied my alignment and tried to correct it, but a classic one-hand balancing would forever remain muscularly hard on me.

On the upside, while fighting for the basics, I was developing qualities no other hand-balancer possessed.

Not only must you think out-of-the-box, but you must realise there is no box. It takes an entirely different mindset, which I had to learn.

I kept working on the skills you must earn to deserve the hand-balancer tag by your name. However, I committed more time to my creativity, always guided by a reliable technique and level of difficulty. I began designing previously unseen shapes with my body, letting go of tags. I did not particularly like the very static feeling of hand-balancing: even masters seemed to parade a set of skills without continuity. What if the routine of incredible movements became a dance on hands, creating a wholesome new language? I had kept my talent in a cage of rules I was forcing on myself. My differences held me back for so long; if I had the guts to let them shine, they might become the tools of my success.

In 2005, I finally dared to launch my first hand-balancing creation. I had designed an apparatus to elevate me from the ground. It would allow me not only to perform on one given spot of the stage but could make the choreography more visually striking by moving around the stage with my props. I had let my peculiar capacities—and incapacities—become instruments to develop a new language on hands. I incorporated a contemporary dance style that would break the expected lines and give even more expression to my body. In the end, my counter-productive long limbs became my signature.

Chapter 16

Imposter syndrome

When you can't access your own fairy-tale.

PHOTOGRAPHY: PIOTRSZALANSKI.PL

Dance on Hands was born. My promotional tool for this creation consisted of the complete eight-minute routine that I filmed in a modest dance studio; no special effects, professional lighting, impressive video editing, or stage sets. I wore the costume I had designed, a perfect hairdo and make-up but still looked like a girl hiding in the basement of a dance school. Maybe it wasn't far from the truth. However, the refinement of my execution oozed something different. Every nanosecond had been considered and rehearsed to perfection. My utmost attention to details was a way for me to feel better about not performing the tricks I thought would earn me respect. I relied on my perfectionism to cover for what I considered my inadequacies.

I sent my demo to artist's agencies, circus companies, theatres, directors, and all of my clients around the world. The response was immediate: international requests and bookings came faster than any of my previous performances.

I liked what I had created, but I still felt I had to apologise for daring to call myself a hand-balancer. I was a total imposter.

The first performance was scheduled not far from Quebec City, on behalf of an important contemporary Canadian circus company sending me to represent them. Oddly, I wasn't looking forward to it, the very same feeling I had felt when I was thirteen, but the cause was different. Until that day, I stepped onstage with confidence, feeling as though I owned the scene. This time, I was nervous; not an adrenaline-fun nervousness but the type of stress that makes you not recognise your own behaviour. I had turned into a wimp. I still pretended I was okay and put on my best face for the rehearsals.

Showtime neared. I was backstage and ready way too early. I had overstretched, overprepared, and exhausted myself trying to be perfect before even stepping onstage—something I learned to pace years later. They delayed my performance by a few minutes as the organisation was running late, which is very common in the event world. This time though, every additional minute of waiting was torture. I had to trick my mind not to let it fall into the fear of failing, literally.

The moment of my big premiere finally arrived.

I step onstage: the place I usually call home. But today I feel naked, flawed, vulnerable like never before. I have built the routine's storyline in six chunks, melted in a choreographic flow, so the audience sees it as a whole. 'If I miss one technical part, I can always do better in the next one,' I repeat to myself. As soon as I climb onto my hands though, I am unprecedentedly shaky; my breathing is restless. It disturbs my balance; the air going in and out of my lungs is doing so in an irregular rock-like feel. Just a few seconds into the routine, I fall. I am not sure I could do it anymore, what is happening to me? Although I was perfect in practice, I feel I have unlearned everything in a matter of seconds. I gracefully camouflage this faux pas and keep going, only to fall again in the second part. After this second mistake, I am ready to run backstage, apologise to the audience, and reimburse the company who had trusted me with their brand. Eventually, I also sabotage the third and the fourth chunk. I make a significant mistake in every single one of the six sections.

A few seconds before the final movement, the audience is silent. I can hear them judging me. I me-ti-cu-lous-ly, carefully… mess up the end. The final note of the music resonates, and the lights fade out. They have just witnessed an elephant trying to stand on tiny branches without a hint of grace.

Do I run away in the dark or stay for the usual bow? When the light comes back for the bow, everyone rises in unison: a standing ovation!

That night, after the show, I was praised for my art, thanked for my talent, and yet I was so disappointed. I stood in my dressing room in silence and eventually packed and went to my hotel. I spent hours flirting with the idea of quitting altogether. The humiliation I felt was unbearable. I had let down the only person I was doing this for, a sense of disgust in my throat.

For the months to come, I worked harder than ever, voluntarily putting myself in stressful situations. I sabotaged a few more shows, but eventually, my technique became solid enough to trust myself. Yet, whenever I was onstage with internationally famous artists for rehearsals, I was intimidated. I knew they expected a world-famous hand-balancer, and here I was with something completely different and—I assumed—inadequate.

MADONNA, BILL CLINTON, AND THE IMPOSTER

I had never been to London, UK. Before rehearsals, I strolled around the streets during a sunny spring day, knowing I needed to keep strength for that night's rehearsals. Towards the end of my planned city tour, it began pouring with rain. I ran down the tube entrance, only to discover that the price of a ticket, with the exchange rate of 2007, equalled the price of a whole dinner in Quebec. I turned around and decided to run back to my hotel. A forty-five minute run under the rain doesn't kill anyone, I thought. I was not wearing appropriate shoes, and my big toenail did not particularly appreciate the experience; I lost part of it. Maybe 12 dollars could have been well invested in keeping my toenail for one of the most important international galas of my career thus far.

I confidently charmed the clients, staff, and crew with my rehearsals, but I was still intimidated that peer performers were watching. Everyone seemed to be the world's best in their field. A surreal water curtain surrounded the round stage on which I performed, creating graphic forms in the air around me. I later learned that the company responsible for the most impressive water shows in Singapore, Las Vegas, and the UAE invented the water marvel around me, and I had to honour their craft with my performance.

The next day, artists had to arrive early at the venue due to the extensive security procedures for what is London's most glamorous charity gala ever seen. Guests arrived on the red carpet. When walking back from the ladies' bathroom, I was slightly confused by where I was: *supermodel land* or *diamond land?* The ticket price was 10,000 pounds sterling to spend an evening in this opulent marquee at Kensington Palace.

My performance was scheduled for right after the opening speech of the evening, followed by Madonna, and after dinner, a singer named Prince.

I am standing behind the curtain that draws the line between billionaires, deep-pocketed civilians, politicians, royalty, and myself. The main room is one of the most stunning designs I've ever seen. I look beautiful in my shiny performance outfit and glamorous bun. 'What a fairy-tale!' screams the story from the outside. But inside, I still don't understand why I am here instead of the best hand-balancer in the world.

The opening speech is heading towards its closing remarks, but I am not listening. The man assisting me tells me to get ready for my entrance. I am standing in my perfect, docile ballerina posture behind the two men who will escort me inside the room. Warm applauses mark the end of the speech. I take a deep breath. We walk towards the stage as the white-haired man who gave the opening speech heads towards us, probably to regain his seat. I suddenly get shadowed by two bodyguards moving quickly. Maybe they just discovered that I'm the imposter of the evening and are going to throw me out of the marquee? Fortunately—or un-fortunately—not. They are only assuring the security of the man who just held the opening speech: Bill Clinton.

I am up next and even more confused.

Onstage, performing between the water graphics flying around me, I catch a glimpse of Elizabeth Hurley's reassuring smile. Madonna's table of dancers is cheering loudly during my whole act.

I manage to dance on my hands like Erika Lemay.

I don't remember anything else from that day, my mind shadowed by a thousand worries of inadequacy. When I was finally escorted outside the venue to get a taxi back to my hotel hours after my performance, paparazzi standing at the door took dozens of photographs. The powerful flash left me disoriented.

'Are you famous?' asked one of them ironically.

I guess we both wish so.

.

16.1

Stop underestimating

Crossing the world for a eureka moment.

F or the next two years, I introduced *Dance on Hands* around the world. I was featured in more and more important events. I presented that piece for two international competitions, each winning an award.

My career was blooming. I was working for royal families, celebrities, and the most important theatres in the world. Cirque du Soleil regularly hired me as a guest performer to launch their shows during national press conferences and featured me during their most important special events.

But when not performing my aerial disciplines, I always had the same feeling of inadequacy, the same anguish.

I was training every day, before the shows, after the shows, daytime, night-time. I still needed to upgrade my skills.

In 2008, I decided to take a few months offstage to dedicate myself to only this purpose. And this time, I needed help. I chose to study where the discipline of hand-balancing difficulty is the highest in the world. For three months, I'd be in rural Beijing, practising eight hours a day with a hand-balancing master, one-on-one training.

I had to refuse promising professional offers and chose the long-term benefits. A part of me also wanted to be disoriented, challenged. I wanted to encounter the pain of working harder than I had ever experienced. I had been craving to be pushed by someone else than myself since my youngest age.

I landed amongst 2,000 Chinese acrobats, most of them children. I was a grown woman with a completely different set of skills and body attributes. The kids found it amusing to compare my skinny legs with theirs, to touch my thin hair. I lived in the students' dorms to experience their reality, a choice I later modified when I discovered we were locked in at night with no way out if a fire broke out, and the cockroaches and I disagreed a little too much for my taste.

When I awoke at six every morning, kids were already training in the main hall and would do so until evening. The respect for their teachers and the rigour was exactly the ambience I had been longing for. The skills I witnessed seemed to belong to another planet. I had seen comparable difficulty levels at international competitions, performed by one or two star Chinese acrobats, but now I discovered hundreds of kids could achieve those levels. It was an acrobatic factory. I was looking forward to my teacher to make me work until I collapsed. I needed to learn the impossible.

My China experience did not go as planned. The teacher was a little lazy and more impressed by my skills than I was of her teaching aptitude. She wanted me to do more of what I already owned. I was a total rock star in this school. They had never seen what I did. They were in awe, wanted me to show off. Sadly, I learned little from them. The teaching technique they used with children couldn't be sustained in adult age without serious injuries. I often saw young men or women, who seemed to be former acrobats, on the campus, now severely injured, sometimes visibly disabled. The lucky ones seemed to become teachers, while others only helped with basic tasks. Most had been separated from their family and lived on the campus since they were little children. They knew nothing else.

Finishing a career at age 18 or 20 and not understanding the outside world was disturbing to me. There was no space for the student to analyse during training. They learned by repeating the same things over and over again with the teacher hitting the part of the body the student needed to correct softly with a wooden stick. How can one learn efficiently if he or she does not understand the learning process? Imagine a world teaching system where analysing would be promoted but the level of repetition as high. In western countries, we would never make a child work as hard; therefore, similar standards are nearly impossible to reach. However, students learn to understand their craft, which is an invaluable tool for self-learning later on and enables a steady improvement curve up for years ahead.

I became an expert in training eight hours a day in silence, having no verbal interaction with anyone for days. My notebook always nearby; I noted everything. I had so much headspace to observe and dissect. During lunch breaks, I would go to the dance room and improvise for the whole hour. I needed to get out of my mental structure. Repeating the same things daily for hours with no space for creativity numbed me. Students were queuing up to peek through the small viewing window into the dance room. I was unaware that I was already world-class; my level was unreachable to them. Aside from learning to live with cockroaches, this experience cured my imposter syndrome. I deserved my place in the spotlight. From there on, I was unapologetically me onstage. I became impermeable to detractors. I stopped hiding my craft. Not only was I a hand-balancer, but I was the *Dancer on Hands*.

I flew to higher success, with the confidence I previously lacked, to deliver a solid performance. When artists I considered my heroes copied my style, I understood how much I had underestimated my craft.

Chapter 17

Forget about trends

Do things by the book, and you'll stay average.

Once you have developed your craft and style, how can you make it visible to the world?

Show business is a flavour-of-week system; if you try to respond to what's fashionable at the moment, you'll end up with a flimsy foundation. When the need of your market and audience changes—and it will continually—you need to reinvent yourself each time. The result is navigating the show business world with a multiple personality disorder.

It is difficult to stand out without an identity.

As an artist, the end begins when we start to produce only to please an audience or client, running after a 'new style', on a hamster wheel, going nowhere.

Don't succumb to the click or likes dictatorship. The same concept applies to live performance; the clapping is the likes and clicks. It doesn't necessarily mean that your craft has an increased value; it means you are showing something that encourages applauses or compels more people to click and like. And this is a slippery slope for some.

You shouldn't need to prepare the audience for what's coming, setting the table for the—let me doubt the very authenticity of it—applause when the best time comes. Instead, aim to surprise them, move them to the core, regardless of the applauses.

Creating is an act of ego; we want to put a part of ourselves out there. We fortify ourselves through this very action. You must have an amount of confidence but especially legitimacy to deliver something worth seeing. Creating what others want is making you a people-pleaser without individuality. It's not sexy. Instead, create for yourself; strive to please yourself. The collateral effect, success, and legacy should be measured on a larger scale. What is the image the world will retain of you in five, 10, 20 years? Keep referring to this question to keep your artistic compass steady. You can't run a marathon with short-term thinking.

To remain imaginative and elite in your field through the years, forget about what people want to see at the very moment. Care about delivering broader concepts through a language. Your style will be your semantic. It needs time to mature and for the audience to assimilate. I don't want to speak my audience's language; I want to teach them mine.

There is an advantage to isolating oneself from what's out in the performance world right now. We are influenced by what we see, consciously or unconsciously. By intentionally removing yourself from the playground, it is easier to remain pure, creatively speaking. The pollution created by a bombardment of images and incredible talents can produce more distraction than inspiration. If your artistry diverts towards the trend of the moment or other people's ideas, it will take you an eternity to get to your destination. The outstanding ones will be talked about years later. You don't need to bother with the temporary noise. When in a creative process, choose total isolation.

I've built an artistic reputation linked to my name, and I stayed true to it. After nearly two decades, I don't have to explain what I do anymore: the images and results speak for themselves.

Your style will evolve over the years. You can innovate but do it within the parameters of your artistic identity. With time, it will rise in value instead of being scattered in different directions. Your craft should be the primary marketing tool. It won't please everyone, but that never mattered in the first place.

MORAL COMPASS

I aspire to live with a solid moral compass in life, constantly questioning myself, my motivations, and purpose. If you do too, your Art should not diverge from these boundaries, especially not for more applause or more likes. It's important to challenge this notion, embracing opportunities to the limit of your artistic values so you can clearly define them. It would be a mistake to go against your moral guideline to fit an external situation. Why would you modify your style to suit a trend or be liked? It is a lack of respect for your Art and yourself. You need to know who you are on and offstage.

As a young artist, it was more challenging to stay on this path. I was receiving attractive offers that I wasn't always 100% comfortable with. I had to think about a few of them thoroughly. Ultimately, by accepting them, I would have done a disservice to my whole life mission. The art of knowing where your limit resides can only be the result of a meticulous thought process. Don't skip it.

As a female contortionist, there is a facility to over-sexualise, not necessarily by removing clothes—nudity can be pure artistry—but in stage attitude. And it can be lucrative early on. This easy win may remove value from the present and future artist to be. If you choose that road as your intended purpose, it's understandable, but I advise thinking this through thoroughly. I knew my direction and potential. However, I can understand a young woman with lower self-esteem or in different circumstances might get side-tracked. Nowadays, one is only a few clicks away from exposing herself or himself in a borderline perverse way, earning a lot of likes but losing a lot in artistic value. Every mistake has first been a choice we made. Your past will follow you, especially if you become known. There are things that can't be unseen by the world around you.

Chapter 18

Double-edged personality traits

Beware of self-sufficient and perfectionist—gone wrong.

PHOTOGRAPHY: JAN DE KONING

I'm a control freak. I like to pilot the ship. I hate to find fault with someone else for a result I could have influenced on my own. In earlier years, I learned to do everything in my field. I was the designer of my costumes, of my image, I studied Canadian and American laws to prepare all the contracts, with specificities of given geographic areas. I was taking care of administration and accounting and always made my own financial decisions for my business. I was not fond of managers, bookers, or anyone else making choices on my behalf. From the age of 13, I was highly attentive to the equipment we used to hang my apparatus in the air and everything technically related (audio, lighting). I learned the knot systems, the working load, and security load of every piece of equipment I hang onto. I took workshops to handle aerial rigging professionally. For years, I was the one hanging my technical gear to the ceiling for a show, even if it was three in the morning the night before a big premiere. I learned video editing and coding for my website—when having a website was innovative. I could be self-sufficient if I wanted.

My control-freak personality made me engage in all the fields interrelated with my craft. But even though I trained so much, I didn't have the right headspace for elite performance. I also filled my days with things I honestly hated doing.

The time you spend taking care of everything but your core expertise will inevitably slow you down on the path to your main goal.

Don't let your days become increasingly filled with responding to urgent matters of secondary importance. To be efficient, you need to value your time and make smarter decisions. Priorities are not necessarily urgent—they're important. The know-how makes you more resourceful, auto-sufficiency is a tool.

Do know how but have the freedom not to do it.

It took me years to learn to delegate. Initially, I considered it a weakness, a lack of responsibility. Like the small child who did not want her dad to cut the meat in small pieces on her plate: I didn't accept much help of any kind, in three-year-old fashion. When I started to respect my time and talent for their real value and took a leap of faith, my quality onstage improved, the creativity multiplied, and my life quality increased.

I can finally say I recovered from my compulsion to read contracts at night or triple-check the logistics of every single booking around the world. I accepted that others could do things better. Mistakes will occasionally occur, but the time I save and energy I can redirect on what matters most is priceless. If you care about quality, the time spent finding the right people to support you will be the most important time spent. Postponing it under the false pretence that you have no time will only delay the results. Create a smart structure in which you delegate to refine your life to the purest expression of your craft.

COWARDLY PERFECTIONIST

Another quality for which I've been praised my whole life but equally slowed me down is my perfectionism. Today I see a negative connotation with this word. Perfectionism is often pure fear wearing pretty make-up.

I'm not talking about striving to do things thoroughly or to high-quality standards, the will to surpass oneself at every moment, aiming for excellence and nothing less. This deserves praise! This is who I choose to be.

Perfectionism though, is the quality of cowards. It easily turns into avoidance, procrastination, and a possible defence mechanism. It is for some of us, a comfort zone. Although reaching a space of perfection might not exist, the pursuit can be reassuring.

You can't be both perfectionist and risk-taking. Taking risks, even calculated, implies a possibility of imperfections. I've kept myself from fantastic opportunities, presuming I still needed to perfect my craft. Perfectionists rarely stand out because they hardly deliver much in a lifetime; they are too busy trying to be perfect, using perfectionism as their protective shield. An artist suffering from it won't present a piece for years because it is not ready, even if it will never be.

I've been guilty of this; I was obsessively consumed by details of lesser importance. I spent hours and hours training on things that seemed so important, only to realise that I had lost years. My perfectionism was procrastination in disguise until I identified it. It is a form of addiction.

By getting too close to details, you cannot see the big picture and use a smart methodology for progress. Instead, keep an eye on the important matter: quality and improvement in relation to time. Perfection should not be a coveted destination but an eternal direction. I see it as a mythical being—it slides through your fingers forever, so you eternally need to progress to feel it. Improvement has no boundaries. Perfecting your craft endlessly is healthy but perfectionism isn't.

Chapter 19

Vulnerability pays off

_____

When it's time to take a risk into the unknown.

PHOTOGRAPHY: LOUISE LEBLANC

A t a certain point in my career, after having worked in a high-end market for years almost exclusively for the elite, I felt disconnected from a real audience. I was invited to perform at the most important parties and productions on the planet, my fee was increasing, clients were happy, but I felt unfulfilled.

Was I becoming ungrateful for where I stood as an artist? I didn't want to feel entitled to success and stop being critical towards myself. I must earn that podium every day. I thought it wasn't the case anymore.

I create my scenario for happiness, fine-tuning continuously during the ride. Never will I accept what *happens* to me. I design my life and choose to keep it intense and extraordinary. I must catch myself when my passion becomes lukewarm. I wasn't as motivated as I had been and had to find out exactly why.

If you're not approaching your work and days with an explosive enthusiasm, it is a sign you must reassess your direction.

ANIMUS FEMINA: SOMETHING TO PROVE TO MYSELF

I had spent a lifetime pushing my body, making my performances spotless down to the millisecond. But I hadn't explored my artistic side to the fullest. I began thinking about a more extended performance. I was craving a deeper connection with my audience. Something that wouldn't limit me to the usual five- to eight-minute moments we can afford to do in such a physically demanding field. But how would it be possible to be onstage for a full-length performance when I felt I was already at 100% capacity during my usual shows? Was it even imaginable without sacrificing the acrobatic level so dear to me? I wouldn't settle for something *pretty*. Without caring about the obstacles, I started obsessively writing, drawing, and dreaming about what would become *Animus Femina*—my first one-woman show.

This new obsession of wanting to perform for a consecutive 75 minutes had become my new threshold. I had to gain the strength, stamina, and endurance to make it happen.

Was it possible?

I did not have a clue.

And did it matter?

I knew I didn't have the mental strength to fail at my new project.

The hours of training, choreography, exploring, and creating would keep me busy every waking hour. I had to hire a director, a choreographer, an assistant, a technical team, a scenographer, and a video content creator. I was trying to control the whole process, wearing every hat, but two weeks before the premiere, my brain short-circuited. I had to let go and focus on what I was best at: being myself onstage. Time was running out, and I had already optimised it to the fullest. I even parked the car a few kilometres from the theatre every morning, so I had to run to work, doing my cardio workout before my day would even start.

The one-woman challenge was real. Even during changes of costumes, hair, and stage sets, I never left the stage. I was hiding under a piece of equipment and reciting a text to the audience while dressing and undressing. It was the first time I wore a microphone during my performances. It gave the spectators a new insight into what I was experiencing, and for me, an added factor to worry about. Through my voice, they could hear me gasp for air, which made me feel even more naked. I had to learn to eliminate the ungraceful sounds I didn't know I produced when in extreme positions. The technicality of hiding a microphone and bodypack transmitter when spinning upside down in small unitard wasn't simple.

After many trials and errors, we designed an undergarment to insert the smallest transmitter on the market between my breasts. But with the rotational gravity of my movements, the bodypack would still move under my costume and disturbed me. The solution was to tape it directly to my sternum. We used duct tape—invented during World War II to keep ammunition dry. It worked marvellously. It also created an impressive bruise. I developed a nasty skin intolerance to the adhesive. I taped the microphone to my collar bone so my hair wouldn't get tangled in it and make me look like the bearded woman in the circus.

The final aerial act unfolds under a curtain of rain. In the transition before, I have to strip off the very well-glued tape from my chest during the trickiest costume change—the skin-rip-off act. Contorting under an enormous piece of fabric on which projections evolve, I create forms with my body in the material. Simultaneously, I strip naked to change into the next costume, which the backstage assistant should leave on a precise spot. The fabric in my face, eyes closed, my hand actively searching for the costume. One day, I realised there was no costume, only floor. My heart skipped a beat before I finally grabbed it, a few centimetres from its usual spot, a few seconds away from a total nakedness disaster.

During my career, I have always performed every piece to perfection a hundred times before presenting them to an audience. This time I had never done the whole show in rehearsals in one go. There was no time. I was fixing problems until the last moment. My manager and the show director had a very heated argument, threatening to leave the project the day before the opening. Fixing the human fighting issues were harder to delegate, I learned.

The first time I was to perform the entire piece without a break would be in front of an audience. The day of the world premiere, I did not know if I could physically do it. Without rest, without water, without stepping offstage from beginning to the end. I was terrified I'd cramp in the middle of the show and have to stop. Or perhaps I wouldn't have time to finish a 30-second costume change before the piece of scenography hiding me revealed my nudity to everyone. Maybe I'd forget the next lines and destroy the whole storyline, making the show incomprehensible.

Eighteen minutes into the 75-minute piece, I hit a wall. This show wouldn't be possible with this mindset. I was anticipating the most difficult acrobatics, mentally repeating the lines coming three minutes later, thinking about my muscles burning, and I needed to spare myself for a movement two scenes ahead. Would I have enough stamina to finish the next five-minute aerial piece? I couldn't even rely on my best friend, muscle memory; the show was too new. While executing life-defying stunts, I had a thousand voices in my head, fighting for immediate attention and action—cacophonic paranoia. At minute 18, I had to put myself in robot mode, my comfort zone—I would execute the *task* but completely miss the purpose of the project. Or, I would risk breaking my patterns.

When I consciously made that choice and shifted into performing emotionally and not mechanically, letting go of the fear of imperfection, something magical happened in me. For the first time in my life, I showed myself at my most vulnerable to the audience. The connection with the public shifted to something more personal. They could feel the pain when the metal hoop slapped me in the ribs at full speed or when I was insecure in the character. I wasn't trying to hide. It was liberating for me and endearing for the audience. They could finally relate to what the principal character in the story was going through and witness a human being.

After the show, applause, and praise, I walked by myself on the backstreets behind the theatre. I understood that it was the culmination of my career. Not for the achievement of having performed an entire one-woman show without fainting, but because I had finally learned to feel a new depth of emotions while performing. A new door had opened. By taking the risks of humiliation and failure, I had let the audience embrace my Art and carry me through it. I had let my body dance me through the process. Until then, I had always been immaculate, unreachable, on a pedestal.

Tears ran down my cheeks.

This experience had been a crash course on humility and vulnerability. Had I known it would have been so taxing physically and emotionally, I would never have started. I'm grateful for the ignorance of the beginner.

I now know the day I became an Artist.

PART 4

Purpose

Chapter 20

What's after climax

The fall back after a big climax is real.

PHOTOGRAPHY: ANTONIO NAPOLI

I'm standing at customs in an airport, and for a second, I don't know which country I am in or where I am going. I look around for signs with a language to refer to, and I see a four-language sign: Switzerland!

The previous night in Russia, I won an international competition I had spent months preparing for. Tonight, I will deliver a spotless performance representing Cirque du Soleil at the most exclusive European-wide broadcast gala. Now, after the show, I am seated in my dressing room whilst the celebrity party is starting. I'm replaying my performance in my head, trying to catch mistakes and planning tomorrow's training. The high of the last weeks is rapidly fading, and the longing is kicking in violently. The void ahead of me feels like knives through my skin.

Over the previous few days, I had performed in Istanbul, Turkey; Venice, Italy; Phoenix, USA; St. Petersburg, Russia; and now I am in Lucerne, Switzerland. Most of my nights were spent on planes. I am not sure when I had last consumed a real meal.

Before every show, however, I felt energised. I couldn't analyse my performances; body memory was in charge. My entire life, I had been training and mentally preparing for moments like these. My brain was feeding on adrenaline, and it felt divine.

How many times have I been seated alone in my hotel room after a phenomenal performance, topping months of exhausting and committed work, only to realise I feel empty?

And now that I had just bowed, here was the sense of emptiness again. I was flying home in a few hours. What would I look forward to now? What would scare me? What would give me the adrenaline I needed to have a reason to wake up in the morning and carry on with my crazy training schedule?

I had just delivered one of the most remarkable performances of my life, and yet I was unable to feel any positive emotions, only a paralysing fear. I could never accept that the rest would be less colourful.

My medicine in these moments had long been to throw myself into an even more extravagant challenge and run after it, chasing the high of excellence again, until I understood it wasn't sustainable. I eventually needed solid ground to land.

How can you prevent the feeling of loss after a significant achievement?

You put so much energy into planning your long-term goals; you also need to plan *the after*. Learn to not fear the feeling of emptiness.

Before you even reach the goal, and while you are still in your go-get-it mindset, take the time to **plan *the post-climax* period**. What will the structure of your days be and your new focus after a positive or negative outcome? Leaving yourself a clean slate might create more void than freedom. Write a plan while you are still busy getting to your peak and only reach for it after going through the next steps. This way, you will know there is something to look forward to on the other side. Establish a timeline according to your knowledge of yourself. I can unplug for three days; after that, I feel that I'm procrastinating.

Pause and restructure. You must take days away from work to gain years of efficiency. That may be counter-intuitive since after finishing a big project and having postponed the rest of life for a while, you will feel like catching up on everything you have neglected in your business and personal life. Pause first; step out of your headspace.

You have to be quiet enough to hear your own voice, and this may seem like an impossible task when the same messages have been running in the background for so long. There is no dopamine and self-worth related to the 'non-achieving' anymore, and that can feel horrible.

Unwire your brain by doing something unrelated to your goals. Art, manual work, socialising—anything that can help the brain switch gears. It will take a few days to tame your mind. Don't panic; it's a normal process. If you are like me and find it impossible to unwind, consider an energetic activity that involves a shift in visual stimulation. For example, a vigorous walk in nature with no contact with the outside world through devices. Neurobiological data has shown that when the gaze is dilated through panoramic vision (for instance, viewing a horizon), you are switching on and off the autonomic nervous system and norepinephrine circuits. This restoring phase will repair your ability to focus on new tasks.

Celebrate. If you never celebrate the successes and milestones, then why are you doing it? It's compelling to dive into the next goal, only to wake up a few years later not even able to remember what you have achieved because you never took time to celebrate the wins and accomplishments. Your mind erases them to leave the space for the next pursuit.

Reward yourself with something that has nothing to do with your craft/work. If you are fully devoted, this may be difficult. It is not a rebound plan or compensation behaviour; it's a way to regain energy and break the pattern deeply ingrained in your mind.

It is odd to plan the unplanning, but boundaries are essential. To remain healthy, rest should have the same limits as excess. While immersed in high-stimuli environments and moments where we are involved with one goal, it's easy to lose the big picture, the deeper purpose.

Finding joy doing something unrelated to a goal is precious. Losing the ability to perceive simple joy, rather than losing adrenaline, is the saddest outcome.

Chapter 21

Can I live without it?

———————————

Only quit on good days.

PHOTOGRAPHY: BOAZ ZIPPOR

'If I can't dance, I'd rather die', she says, without any irony. In the documentary *Restless Creature*, ballerina Wendy Whelan, already in her forties, is faced with the probability of having to stop dancing. These words hit me like a train at full speed. I realised that I could—at some point in my life—relate to what she had just said.

For years, I've known this stage career would end. Everything I had been doing from the age of four would suddenly vanish from my daily life and only exist in videos and photographs. This depressing thought has been haunting me for a long time.

I've lived for art and performances my whole life. Extreme emotions, creativity, and overcoming physical boundaries make me feel alive. Within this career and the lifestyle that comes with it, I could bear nothing ordinary. I find the utmost comfort in challenges and extremes.

How could anything else not translate into a lukewarm existence? I was desperately looking for something that could make my life valuable in the future. Never would I accept referring to myself as the person I had once been, surfing on my past achievements.

'You must be looking forward to your retirement, not having to make these sacrifices every day, being able to rest and take time for yourself,' they kept saying.

Time for myself has always been through my Art; it fulfilled me; it thrilled me. I love this life I have built and the fast pace that comes with it! There are no sacrifices, only choices I make every day.

As my mid-thirties approached, my craft was still improving, and I owed it all the attention in the world. After decades of refining my skills, I finally knew my body enough to use it in the most extraordinary ways. My level of subtlety was nothing like that of a

25-year-old. My career kept flourishing in an even more exciting direction. There was so much ahead of me; so many ideas and goals still to fulfil. The threat of one day having to stop was nonetheless present. I was feeding interests and ventures on the side to prepare for that future, but nothing ever came close to moving me in the way my Art did. It remained clear—my profound love and passion were being onstage, improving my *Physical Poetry*, and sharing it with the world. I could not envisage this part of me being taken away.

Until life held that gun to my head.

On my back, facing the background screens, I don't feel my left upper body the way I usually do. I gaze at my left shoulder and don't like what I see.

Three thoughts pass through my head, in chronological order, in a matter of seconds:

The audience must have noticed.

I've had an incredible stage career.

I am deformed. Will I now be handicapped?

The music keeps playing as I lay on the floor; seconds seem like an eternity. The blue and amber projectors are still hitting my acrobatic props, though my body now lays in the dark. My right hand holds my left shoulder as if it wanted to protect it from something that has already happened. I'm conscious, too conscious. . .

Looking at her still dancing on her hands. Because she would never stop.

ONLY QUIT ON GOOD DAYS.

I would not accept this as the conclusion to my career. After the surgery and months of rehabilitation, all sense of physical pride was a ridiculous concept to me. My abilities had shifted from impossible acrobatics in the sky to attempting to lift my arm slightly with the help of a wall. I had to trick myself into turning it into a learning experience. It was my new anatomy class; my nervous system teaching me sensations I couldn't relate to. I needed that change of viewpoint to not judge myself when I struggled with the easiest tasks. As physical performers, we spend hours every day practising in front of mirrors or watching videos of ourselves, trying to fix the slightest visual imperfections—a narcissistic power the body I now possessed could no longer afford.

After months of fighting for any signs of improvement, I gradually began to train like an athlete again. I lost the weight I had gained from immobile hours on a medical bed, having my inner muscles stimulated with needles. Very slowly, I regained part of my muscle mass on the scary meagre arm, attached to my trunk with what looked nothing like a shoulder. Although it was still hard to hold a fork or a teacup, I wanted to physically return to my previous self, in the body I felt I belonged. A year after the accident, I committed to performing again, 25 metres in the sky.

As elite performers, happy is not the main quest—happy happens when we achieve. We learned to feel merely through the performance euphoria or a breakthrough during training. Adrenaline is our fuel. When the fuel is flying above a cheering crowd of 25 thousand, touring the world as the featured guest on TV shows, and dipping toes daily into the celebrity lifestyle, the gap might be difficult to fill. My worst fear was never to feel that high again, through anything other than performing onstage.

I don't believe that things happen for a reason. I believe things happen.

And we have to deal with even the most traumatic happenings in the best way we can. But if things did happen for a reason, the accident would have rid me of the false belief that intensity resided in my performing Art. It was in me the whole time, and I only had to find a way to feel it. Performing was a means, not an end.

When I landed on the floor safely after my first performance post-accident, one thing was clear: I was ready to turn the page and close that chapter. My priorities had shifted and not towards something dull.

I have learned many different angles of my Art—directing, creating, producing, but never with the commitment I had applied to my life as a stage performer. After a year of exploring the possibilities of a life strictly offstage, I dug deeper into the creative arena, a place where I previously wore blinders. I had to make space to realise everything I can change and improve around me.

So, the question remained. How could I survive without my Art?

I wouldn't have to. I was mistaking something for death that was about to be born.

That year offstage had been a learning experience on steroids. Nothing about it had been lukewarm. The intensity I felt in my performing career was one I could take wherever I go. Getting better remains my prime focus but through a new voice.

My body was a means of transportation for my Art and purpose, a tool. It is breakable.

I am not.

In hindsight, maybe my career was slowing down my ambition and not the other way round. I had built invisible walls, and I was living within the boundaries of my craft. I could finally create with *Physical Poetry*'s language but through different mediums and artists, conducting a symphony of visual beauty instead of one instrument.

I had made a promise to myself: to leave the stage at my peak. A concept one can unfairly manipulate. The risk is to notice only after you have long fallen. The rising is never steady—it's a continuity of ups and downs with a constant general upward. How do I know the peak is behind me when my eyes are always on something higher?

Then I thought I'll leave when I have nothing to give anymore, which is a paradox. How could I someday become so boring that I've said it all?

It's time to leave when you have more to give elsewhere.

I had the extreme luck of Karine entering my life as she was about to exit hers. She took my hand and led me towards what would become not only my livelihood but my true passion. She was what people call destiny. And now it was my turn. We guide our destiny, some softly, others with a leash. I have years to master it.

Let the fun begin!

Chapter 22

Redefining yourself

*How to let go of the old you
and redefine the future.*

I'm in Atlanta, still very nervous to perform on behalf of this multinational entertainment company. A new client. . . I have to impress. After the show, my artistic director knocks on the door of my dressing room. The CEO wants to congratulate me. He can't hide his enthusiasm; neither can my artistic director. Despite decades in the performing business, he has never seen such performance. He will hire me again.

About an hour later. I am packing my equipment in the corridor close to the kitchen of the ballroom. A waitress timidly comes closer, stepping away from her colleagues.

'I apologise for the intrusion', she says in her Ukrainian accent.

'I just saw your performance, and I have a request for you'.

Her eyes are glassy; she clears her throat. She hesitates one moment, then continues. 'Never ever stop. What you do gives hope to people, water for my thirsty soul. Thank you. Thank you. Thank you'.

She disappears.

I will never forget this moment. That's why I do what I do. Not to impress CEOs and celebrities, although it's flattering. I do this to move people.

HOW TO LET GO

You can't create the most extraordinary life by hanging onto the old one.

The transition athletes go through has been documented, researched by psychologists, and displayed in the media every single post-Olympics month. You have to mourn, embrace a softer life, they say. You married something through heaven and hell, and you did go through both; the emotional attachment is intense. How can we then ask ourselves to be content with the ordinary?

But doesn't everyone who has a passion with an expiry date—through which they live veraciously—eventually have to go through the same detachment and mourning? The difference is that as a physical performer, the body decides and the mind often isn't at peace with it, even if we spend years pretending to be. We can stretch the end, able to bear more pain, put in more effort for the same physical outcomes, or even have more surgeries. At some point, it's time for that last bow.

So many dancers, athletes, and physical performers feel disoriented or without an identity when they end their career. They crafted their personality within the boundaries of their sports and art. They have spent more time with their coaches and colleagues than any of their family members, even in the most formative years.

You evolve into an environment that helps you plan, think, do. There is a village crafted around you, and you step in without too many questions. You follow the program and concentrate on your role in it.

That's where my chance resided. I built my village and remained an independent thinker. I've never felt like a misplaced element of a larger structure. Of course, it is challenging for me to make that shift in my life, and at times, very painful. However, by having held the strings of my career and its different components, I became a conductor with a much more significant role than if I had done what I was told to do until it was over and my place in the system suddenly became irrelevant.

There were dominos—artistic, physical, agenda, clientele, health—I had carefully placed, one at a time, understanding the components and keeping a delicate equilibrium to evolve in the highest quality. I knew of the house of cards I was living in; it eventually fell. But there was a solid foundation under it, of significant value and self-investment.

Only if you understand by learning the system and not just executing will you have the chance to build something even better on your own. Don't seek deniability; you inherit what you create. You learn nothing by delegating fault. Your default thinking pattern should be that it's your responsibility.

How do you let go of the old representation of yourself to deep dive into a new chapter?

In times of transition, avoid fooling yourself with shiny objects. Question your motivation and purpose daily. Take time to ponder a few essentials about your past, present, and future so you do not fall into a romanticised version of the new or lost possibilities. Learn where the new borders are and where passions merge.

Nostalgia has no role to play in the story of your future.

PAST

- What were the best moments of your career? Not the ones that gave you a high at the moment and then faded away, such as performing in front of millions, but the moments you'll remember 20 years from now.
- What is the most painful to let go of? Are you attached to the glory and lifestyle, or is it a physiological response you can't do without? Identify what it is that makes it hard to let go. You can replicate these components in a new system.
- What is the easiest to let go of? There are always things we hate in something we love. Remember these parts, and when you need to mourn a past life, include it in the picture. I do not miss the constant pain of overusing my body or the countless tendinosis I had to live with.

PRESENT

- What do you live for? What is your primary motivator in life?
- You will probably come up with a mishmash of unrelated information. Remove the less important one by one until the key points remain. Stripping it down to the essentials expresses so much more.
- If happiness was a currency, what concrete action would give you the best return on investment?
- Without taking any results into consideration, what do you like learning or doing the most?

FUTURE

- Describe how you want to spend your days for decades to come.
- Imagine you look back on your life, right before signing off—what will you be proud of? (This can be something you still have not explored).

Find where these answers align; that's your compass.

My answers converged towards the same place: *Create beauty to inspire the world. Push boundaries through an active, culturally and intellectually rich life.*

REDEFINING YOURSELF

You have a particular personality, experience, and acquired skills. You don't need a definition for others to see; you need to know who you are.

As a performer, you achieve a certain status—people look up to your prowess, they venerate the life you lead. It never bothered me, what other people thought, but I noticed that I did appreciate the status it gave me towards myself. That's something I would first have to push in the background. Not only did I grow proud of my craft, but I became intimately bonded to it, at times confusing it with who I was.

Your craft is a result, not a core foundation. You can create anew countless times. What you achieved over the years is a mirror of your personality and a fraction of what you can become.

You will find in every single profession half-hearted individuals and absolutely passionate ones. Personality matters so much more than we think. Don't let changing circumstances threaten your identity. What you do is not what you are, but a testimony of your potential. On the other hand, what you are can influence everything you do.

You can use what you have learned through past experiences to produce what you want in the future. It might have taken you 25 years to sharpen your skills, but now you can apply them to different fields or the same area in countless ways if you choose to. Skills can be transferred.

Don't look at a new chapter as a plan B. It might be the plan A you weren't ready to see.

If you dare to dream, then dream big and make your future intimidating to your past. You can change the world with Art, opening emotional gates in others no words would reach. Art is a human act. If selfless, it changes lives.

Care to make a difference.

Acknowledgments

Some individuals on the Almost Perfect rollercoaster of creation have been irreplaceable. First and foremost, David L. Hancock, Bonnie Rauch, and the whole team at Morgan James Publishing; you've proven that with the right teamwork, magic can happen. I am beyond grateful that our paths collided. Special thanks to Wendy J. Hall from GrayHorse Expressions and Luschka van Onselen for having helped me fine-tune my voice and for your graceful patience in facing my obsession with details. Wild gratitude to Justin Rose, Antonio Fazio, Marlise McCormick, Filippo Ongaro, Derek Sivers, Nina Verdelli, and Françoise Kirkland for your honest feedback. The late Clément Legendre and Micheline Sévigny; you so gracefully honoured Karine by the way you lived. Your strength and generosity have inspired me throughout this journey and beyond. Andréanne Quintal for your boundless support. René Allemann for making me fly higher, once more.

.

About the author

An internationally awarded artist and public personality, **Erika Lemay** has become a beautifully disruptive icon in the world of live performance. She is the creator of *Physical Poetry*; a form of art that gained her worldwide recognition and accolades. Since the age of 11, Erika has performed on the most prestigious stages around the globe and extensively as a soloist guest star with Cirque du Soleil.

PHOTOGRAPHY:
LAZARINA KANOROVA

Her TV performances have been seen by more than 400 million viewers worldwide, and her talent has been featured in international medias, including Vanity Fair, Glamour Magazine, Hello Magazine, Le Figaro, and La Repubblica. Vanity Fair Italia nominated Erika as the New Queen of Circus in an interview featuring exclusive pictures by legendary photographer and Hollywood icon-maker Douglas Kirkland, who's latest book, *Physical Poetry Alphabet*, is a tribute to her work. Erika is living proof that work ethic and daily discipline give one the freedom to live an extraordinary life. Today she is a coveted show director and public speaker, but above all, an unclassifiable artist. She lives with the love of her life, between Lisbon, Portugal, and Zurich, Switzerland.

A free ebook edition is available with the purchase of this book.

To claim your free ebook edition:

1. Visit MorganJamesBOGO.com
2. Sign your name CLEARLY in the space
3. Complete the form and submit a photo of the entire copyright page
4. You or your friend can download the ebook to your preferred device

A **FREE** ebook edition is available for you or a friend with the purchase of this print book.

CLEARLY SIGN YOUR NAME ABOVE

Instructions to claim your free ebook edition:
1. Visit MorganJamesBOGO.com
2. Sign your name CLEARLY in the space above
3. Complete the form and submit a photo of this entire page
4. You or your friend can download the ebook to your preferred device

Print & Digital Together Forever.

Snap a photo

Free ebook

Read anywhere